THE L♥VER'S DICTIONARY

HOW TO BECOME AMOROUS IN FIVE DELECTABLE LANGUAGES

by the editors of Passport Books

BELL PUBLISHING COMPANY

New York

Preface

So you're going abroad!

So you want to have a good time.

So you're out to prove that Don Juan was a little leaguer.

So you did the right thing in spending a few bucks on this handy book.

Let's face it, Lover Boy, your reputation is not so hot with European and Latin women. You are too obvious, too aggressive, too insensitive, too impatient,...too everything in lovemaking. To make matters worse, you want to make love like you do everything else, in *English!*

Now, with this handy *Lover's Dictionary,* you can learn to be as subtly suggestive as the Frenchman, as carefree as the Italian, as romantic as the Spaniard, or as attentive as the German—in a matter of minutes!

This unbelievable little book will make you an instant lover in French, Spanish, Italian and German!

The Lover's Dictionary is simplicity itself. It's arranged in such a way that you can quickly master snappy phrases for use on a plane, train or boat, then moves into everyday situations for restaurants, night clubs, hotels, etc. With each translation is a simple phonetic spelling of each expression. Even if you don't sound like a native, the lady you're pursuing will understand (then you're on your own!)

Here are some tips from the guys and gals who dared to research this book:

1. Don't pass yourself off as fluent in French, or Italian, or Spanish, or German, or *any* foreign language. Women spot a phony instantly and they'll leave you cold!

2. Show your newfound lady friend that you're trying. Matter of fact, refer to the *Dictionary* in her presence. She'll love you more for trying.

3. Be prepared for rejection, a slap in the face, or worse. Reflect on what you did wrong (like did you try to proposition a guy's wife right in front of him?). If necessary, hit back—with your *Dictionary* (note the heavy paper and binding).

4. Let nothing stop you! Go forward! Charge! We want you to return home like Caesar did. Remember? Veni (Vehnee), Vidi (Veedee), Vinci (Vinkee)! Happy hunting!

The Editors
PASSPORT BOOKS

A WORD TO WOMEN FROM THE EDITORS

Is this book chauvinistic? Perhaps. However, we see it differently. The American male has been losing the race in international lovemaking. In fact the poor slob is losing out on the home front as foreign Romeos invade our turf and steal our beauties. It's time to fight back! This book is a small offering to help restore the American male as a major contender in international lovemaking. If you are a free-spirited woman, buy this book for your guy to take along on his next foreign trip and watch him return like the tiger he once was.

P.S. You, too, will find this book effective in fighting off (or encouraging) those suave continental lovers. And with this book, you're in charge. You get what you want, when *you* want it. And that's not bad, n'est-ce pas?

NOTES ON PRONUNCIATION
by the translators

FRENCH. Gallic polysyllabic fluency comes hard to the American, accustomed as he is to being a man of few words. French vowels, uttered with the force of a minor explosion, come hard too. And in the state of high passion in which we hope readers of this book will find themselves, there will be neither time nor inclination to ponder deeply on pronunciation. We have, therefore, altered some French sounds to try to make them similar to English vowels. (If said pretty quickly, they almost sound like the real thing.) Here are a few notes that will help in reading the phonetic version:

Where there is 'u' in French, or 'ure', the u has been replaced by i. This must be pronounced as in 'bit' and not as in 'bite'.

The French 'j' has been translated by 'sh', but this must be pronounced fairly lightly. The word 'garage' has this sound.

The 'e', 'eu' and 'eur' sounds are expressed as 'er' or 'ehr'. Quite easy, if you lengthen them a bit. 'Euse' has been put as 'ehrz'.

Liaisons have been put in as being part of the word, in almost every case.

The 'ail' sound was the hardest to translate—'ay' dare not be used in case it was pronounced as in 'may'—so, it was decided to use 'aee' or 'a'ee'—but the ee must not be stressed.

'En', 'em', 'in', 'im', 'ein' and 'un' have all been translated by 'an' or 'am'. You can get away with it in the heat of the moment.

'Oi' by 'w', of course. Easy.

Finally, all would-be French speakers are reminded that in this delightful language all words are stressed on the last syllable, whatever the length.

GERMAN. The German double letter 'ß' is replaced here by 'ss'. Other usages are:

ch:	pronounce hard as in loch
g:	pronounce hard as in good
i:	read always short as in 'fit'
y:	like 'fly'
ao:	as in 'owl'

ITALIAN. The Italian translator has produced his own system of phonetics, which should stand the one-language American in good stead. He reminds you that in Italian every vowel is pronounced.

SPANISH. *á* or *ah* is pronounced as the English *a* in *car*. (Never like *all, dare, gave*.)
é or *eh* is always like the English *e* in *set, let, wet*. (Never like *me, here, become*.)
ó or *oh* has the sound of English *o* in *lord* or English *aw* in *law*. (Never like *old, go, ago*.)
i has the sound of *i* in *bit*. (Never of *I, mine, island*.)
y has the sound of *y* in *yes, yawn*, or the *e* in *me*. (Never like *my, by, cry*.)
th has the sound of English *th* in *thing*. (Never of *the, that, this*.)

SPECIAL NOTE. As in *THE INSULT DICTIONARY* the translations are intended to give local equivalents or to express the same understandable idea, not to give mere literal equivalents that may mean nothing to the other person.

CONTENTS

ON BOARD SHIP

Please excuse me—wrong cabin.

O, Verzeihung—falsche Kabine!

(O, fertsy-oong—faalshe cabine.)

Actually, I'm traveling incognito.

Ehrlich gestanden, ich reise inkognito.

(Erlish geshtaanden, ish ryze incognito.)

I grabbed you because I thought you needed some help.

Ich dachte, ich sollte Sie festhalten.

(Ish daachte, ish zolte zi festhaalten.)

Where am I? I must be sleepwalking.

Wo bin ich? Nachtwandele ich?

(Vo bin ish? Naacht-vaandle ish?)

Honestly, these pills are just for seasickness.

Wirklich, diese Pillen sind nur gegen Seekrankheit.

(Virklish, dise pillen zind noor gaygen zaykraankhyt.)

Oh, pardon! Je me suis trompé de cabine.	Scusi, ho sbagliato cabina.	Perdone. Me he equivocado de camarote.
(Oh pardon! Sherm swee trompay der cabeen.)	*(Skoo-zy oh sbah-lee-ah-toh kah-bee-nah.)*	*(Perdóneh. Meh eh ekkiboccádoh deh kahmahróteh.)*
A vrai dire, je voyage incognito.	Veramente viaggio in incognito.	Realmente, viajo de incógnito.
(Ar vray deer, sher vwahyash anconeeto.)	*(Veh-rah-menteh vee-ah-joh een in-koh-nee-toh.)*	*(Reh-alménteh, beeyáhho deh eencógnitoh.)*
J'ai cru que vous aviez besoin d'aide.	Credevo che avesse bisogno di appoggio.	Creí que iba a caerse.
(Shay cri ker voo zavyay berzwan daid.)	*(Creh-deh-voh keh ah-vehs-seh bee-zoh-nee-oh dee ap-poh-joh.)*	*(Kreh-ee ké eebah ah kahérseh.)*
Où suis-je? J'ai dû avoir encore une crise de somnanbulisme.	Dove sono? Devo essere sonnambulo.	¿Dónde estoy? ¡Debo ser sonámbulo!
(Oo sweesh? Shay di ahvwar ankor in creez der somnanbileezm.)	*(Doh-veh soh-noh? Deh-voh esseh-reh son-nahm-boo-loh.)*	*(Dóndeh stóy? Déboh sér sonámbooloh!)*
Je vous jure que ces pilules sont contre le mal de mer.	L'assicuro, queste pillole sono soltanto per il mal di mare.	¡Palabra! Estas píldoras son sólo contra el mareo.
(Sher voo shir ker say peelil son contr ler mal der mair.)	*(Lahs-see-koo-roh, kwehsteh pilloh-leh soh‧noh per eel mahl dee mah-reh.)*	*(Pahlábrah! Éstass peeldórass són sóloh kóntrah él mahréh-oh.)*

ON BOARD SHIP

You should see the view from my cabin.

Von meiner Kabine hat man eine bessere Aussicht.

(Fon myner cabine haat maan yne bessere aosisht.)

It's my birthday; just have one drink with me.

Trinken Sie doch wenigstens ein Gläschen mit mir—heute ist mein Geburtstag.

(Trinken zi doch venigstens yn glays-shen mit mir—hoyte ist myn geboortstag.)

ON THE PLANE

I'm sorry, I was just looking for my seat belt.

O, Verzeihung, ich wollte meinen Sicherheitsgurt festschnallen.

(O, fertsy-oong, ish volte mynen zisherhyts-goort festshnallen.)

Do you mind holding my hand? Takeoffs scare me to death.

Würden Sie bitte meine Hand halten? Ich habe Angst vor dem Aufsteigen.

(Vuerden zi bitte myne haand haalten? Ish haabe aangst for daym aofshtygen.)

Venez dans ma cabine, on a une de ces vues . . . !	Dalla mia cabina c'è una vista molto piú bella.	Hay mejores vistas desde mi camarote.
(Vernay dan ma cabeen, on ar in der say vi . . . !)	*(Dahl-lah mee-ah kah-bee-nah cheh oo-nah vee-stah mohl-toh pew bel-lah.)*	*(Áy mehhóress beestass dés-deh mee kahmahróteh.)*
C'est mon anniversaire, venez donc boire juste un verre avec moi.	Prenda qualcosa da bere con me—è il mio comple-anno.	Es mi cumpleaños. Venga a tomar un trago conmigo.
(Say mon aneevairsair, ver-nay donk bwar shist an vair aveck mwar.)	*(Prehn-dah kwal-koh-zah dah beh-reh kon meh—eh eel mee-oh kom-pleh-ahn-noh.)*	*(Ess mee koompleh-ányoss. Béngah ah tohmárr oon trágoh kón-meegoh.)*
Je m'excuse, j'essayais de boucler la ceinture.	Scusi, stavo cercando di allacciare la cintura del sedile.	Lo siento. Quería apretar mi cinturón de seguridad.
(Sher mexkiz, shessayay der booklay la santir.)	*(Skoo-zy, stah-voh cher-can-doh dee allah-chee-ah-reh lah cheen-too-rah dehl seh-dee-leh.)*	*(Loh seeyéntoh. Kehreeyáh aprehtárr mee thintoorón dé segooreedáth.)*
Gardez ma main dans la vôtre, je vous prie, je suis terrifié chaque fois que l'avion va décoller.	Le dispiace tenermi la mano? Ho tanta paura al momento del decollo.	¿Le importaría darme la mano? Me asusta mucho despegar.
(Garday ma man dan la votr, sher voo pree, sher swee terreefyay shack fwar ker lavyon va daicolay.)	*(Leh dee-spee-ah-cheh teh-ner-mee lah mah-noh? Oh tahn-tah pah-oo-rah ahl momentoh dehl deh-kol-loh.)*	*(Leh importareeya dármeh lá mánoh? Meh assoostah mootchoh despehgárr.)*

ON THE PLANE

I don't know where to go in _____, and I don't know anyone there.

Ich kenne niemanden hier und weiss auch nicht, wo es 'lang geht.

(Ish kenne nimaanden heer oond vys aoch nisht, vo es laang gayt.)

If you lift the armrest we'll both be more comfortable.

Nehmen Sie die Armlehne zwischen uns 'raus, das ist bequemer.

(Naymen zi di armlayne tsvishen oons 'raos, daas ist bequaymer.)

If you lift the armrest we'll both be more comfortable.

FRENCH	ITALIAN	SPANISH

Je ne connais personne à
_____ et je ne sais où aller.

*(Shern conay pairson ar
_____ ay shern say oo
allay.)*

A _____ non conosco
nessuno, e non so proprio
dove andare.

*(Ah ...... non coh-noh-
skoh neh-soo-noh eh non soh
proh-preeoh doh-veh ahn-
dah-reh.)*

No conozco a nadie ni sé
donde ir en _____.

*(Noh konóthkoh ah náddye
nee sé dóndeh eer én ......)*

Si on relevait l'accoudoir
du milieu, ce sera plus
confortable!

*(See on rehlvay lacoodwar
di meelyer, ser srah pli
confortahbl!)*

Togliamo il bracciolo di
mezzo—è tanto piú comodo
senza.

*(Toh-lee-ah-moh eel brah-
chee-oh-loh dee metzoh—
eh tahn-toh pew koh-moh-
doh sen-tzah.)*

Quite el apoyabrazos cen-
tral, se está más cómodo.

*(Keeteh él ahpóyah-bráthoss
zentrál, sé stá máss
kómodoh.)*

ON THE TRAIN

Excuse me, is this seat taken?

Entschuldigen Sie, Fräulein, ist dieser Platz noch frei?

(Entshooldigen, zi, fräulyn, ist diser plaats noch fry?)

I'm sorry; this train is bouncing so much I can't keep out of your seat.

Tut mir leid, aber der Zug schaukelt immer nach dieser Seite.

(Toot mir lyd, aaber der tsoog shaokelt immer naach diser syte.)

I hope you can squeeze me in.

Da ist doch bestimmt noch eine kleine Lücke frei.

(Daa ist doch beshtimmt noch yne klyne luecke fry.)

You look too young to be traveling alone.

Sie sind doch viel zu jung, um schon allein zu reisen. Sind Sie schon sechzehn?

(Zi zind doch fil tsoo yoong, oom shon allyn tsoo ryzen. Zind zi shon zayshtsayn?)

FRENCH	ITALIAN	SPANISH
Excusez-moi, s'il vous plaît, est-ce que cette place est prise? (*Exkizay-mwar, seel voo play, esker set plahs ay preez?*)	Scusi signorina, è occupato quel posto? (*Skoo-zy see-nee-oh-ree-nah, eh ok-koo-pah-toh kwel poh-stoh?*)	Perdone, señorita, ¿está ocupado este asiento? (*Perdónneh, senyoreetah, stá okoopádoh ésteh assyéntoh?*)
Je m'excuse, mais je ne peux empêcher le mouvement du train de me jeter vers vous. (*Sher mexkiz, may shern perzampaishay ler moovman di tran der mer shertay vair voo.*)	Mi scusi tanto ma è il movimento del treno che mi spinge contro di lei. (*Mee skoo-zy tan-toh mah eh eel moh-vee-men-toh dehl treh-noh keh mee speen-jeh kon-troh dee leh-ee.*)	Lo siento, el tren se balancea hacia su lado. (*Loh seeyéntoh, él trén seh balanthéah áthiah soo ládoh.*)
J'espère que vous voudrez bien vous serrer un peu pour me faire une petite place. (*Shaispair ker voo voodray byan voo serray an per poor mer fair in perteet plahs.*)	Me lo fa un posticino piccolo piccolo? (*Meh loh fah oon poh-stee-chee-noh pick-koh-loh pick-koh-loh?*)	Espero que pueda apretarse un poquito más. (*Spéroh ké pwéddah aprehtárseh oon pokeetoh máss.*)
Vous êtes bien trop jeune pour voyager toute seule—vous n'avez même pas seize ans, je parie? (*Voozait byan tro shern poor vwayahshay too serl—voo navay maim par saizan, sher paree?*)	Mi sembra troppo giovane per viaggiare da sola—ha compiuto sedici anni? (*Mee sehm-brah trop-poh joh-vah-neh per vee-ah-jah-reh dah soh-lah: ah compee-oo-toh seh-dee-chee ahn-nee?*)	Parece muy joven para viajar sola . . ¿Ha cumplido ya dieciséis años? (*Parétheh mooy hóben párah beeyahhár sólah . . . Ah koompleedoh yáh dyéthisséis ányoss?*)

ON THE TRAIN

Aren't you _____?

Sind Sie nicht _____?

(Zind zi nisht _____?)

My eyes hurt; may I turn out the light?

Meine Augen vertragen das Lich nicht; darf ich es ausknipsen?

(Myne aogen fertraagen das lish nisht; daarf ish es aoscknipzen?)

Let me help you with your suitcase.

Erlauben Sie—darf ich mit Ihren Gepäck helfen?

(Erlaoben zi, daarf ish mit irer gepeck helfen?)

I'm sorry, but it's so crowded I couldn't move my hands if I wanted to.

Tut mir leid, es ist nicht möglich, meine Hände wegzunehmen in diesem Gedränge.

(Toot mir lyd, es ist nisht moeglish myne hande vaigtsoonemen in dizem gedraynge.)

Let me sleep on the floor of your compartment. I won't be in the way.

Darf ich nicht in Ihrem Schlafwagen auf dem Fussboden liegen—das stört Sie doch sicherlich nicht.

(Daarf ish nisht in irem schlaaf-vaagen aof dem fossboden ligen—das shtoert zi doch zisherlish nisht.)

FRENCH	ITALIAN	SPANISH
Vous ne seriez pas_____ _____ par exemple? (*Voon sehryay par _____, pahr exampl?*)	Ma lei non è _____? (*Mah leh-ee non eh_____ _____?*)	¿No es usted _____? (*Noh ess oosté _____?*)
Cette lumière me fatigue un peu les yeux, vous permettez que j'éteigne? (*Set limyair mer fateeg an per laiz yer, voo pairmetay ker shettain?*)	Mi bruciano gli occhi— posso spenger la luce? (*Mee broo-chee-ah-noh lee ock-kee—poh-soh spehn-jer lah loo-cheh?*)	Me duelen los ojos, ¿puedo apagar la luz? (*Meh dwéllen loss óhhoss, pwéddoh apahgárr lah looth?*)
Laissez-moi vous aider à placer votre valise. (*Laissay-mwar voo zaiday ar plahsay votr valeez.*)	Permetta che l'aiuti con la valigia. (*Per-met-tah keh lah-yew-tee kohn lah vah-lee-jah.*)	Permítame que la ayude con sus paquetes. (*Permeetah-meh ké lah ah-yoodeh kón soos packétess.*)
Je m'excuse, mais il y a tellement de monde que je ne peux même pas bouger les mains. (*Sher mexkiz, maizeelyar tellman der mond ker shern per maim par booshay lay man.*)	Mi dispiace, ma siamo così pigiati che non riesco a muovere le mani. (*Mee deespee-ah-cheh, mah see-ah-moh koh-zy pee-jah-tee keh non ree-eh-skoh ah moo-oh-veh-reh leh mah-nee.*)	Lo siento, pero hay tanta gente que no puedo quitar de ahí las manos. (*Loh seeyéntoh, péroh áy tántah hénteh ké nó pwéddoh keetár dé ah-ee lass mánoss.*)
Je vais rester par terre dans votre couchette, comme ça je ne vous gênerai pas. (*Sher vay restay pahr terr dan votr cooshet, com sah shern voo shainray par.*)	Lasci che mi metta per terra nel suo vagone letto— non le darò nessuna noia. (*Lah-shee keh mee met-tah per ter-rah nehl soo-oh vah-goh-neh let-toh—non leh dah-ròh nes-soo-nah noh-ee-ah.*)	Déjame quedar debajo de tu litera. No te molestaré. (*Déhhameh keddár debáhho dé too leetérah. Nó té molesstáréh.*)

Excuse me, is this $_____bill yours?

Verzeihen Sie bitte, gehört der _____markschein Ihnen?

(Fertsyn zi bitte, gehurt der _____-markshyn inen?)

Where can I find the Lonely Hearts Club in this town?

Können Sie mir den Weg zum Club Einsamer Herzen zeigen?

(Koennen zi mir dayn vayg tsoom cloob ynzamer hairtsen tsygen?)

I didn't mean to bump into you.

Entschuldigung, das war nicht meine Absicht.

(Endshooldigoong, daas vaar nisht myne upsisht.)

I'm sorry, I mistook you for_____.

Verzeihung, ich habe Sie mit Elisabeth Taylor verwechselt.

(Fertsy-oong, ish haabe zi mit _____ fervayxelt.)

Hello, Beautiful!

Hallo, Prachtstück!

(Hallo, praacht-shtuek.)

FRENCH	ITALIAN	SPANISH

Excusez-moi, il est à vous ce billet de _____?

(Exkizay-mwar, eel aitar voo ser beeyayd____?)

Scusi, è sua questa banconota?

(Skoo-zee eh soo-ah kwestah ban-ko-noh-tah?)

Perdona, ¿ es tuyo este billete de _____ pesetas?

(Perdónah, éss tooyoh ésteh billyéteh dé _____ pessétass?)

Pouvez-vous m'indiquer où se trouve le club des cœurs solitaires?

(Poovay-voo mandeekay oo ser troov ler clerb day ker soleetair?)

C'è un locale dove un povero cane solitario può trovare un po' di compagnia?

(Chèh oon local-eh doh-veh oon poh-veh-roh cah-neh solitar-eeoh pwo troh-vah-reh oon poh dee compah-nee-ah?)

¿Puedes decirme dónde está el club de los corazones solitarios?

(Pwéddes dethirmeh dóndeh stá él cloob dé lóss korathóness solitáryoss?)

Je n'ai pas fait exprès.

(Sher nay par fay expray.)

L'assicuro non era mia intenzione urtarla.

(Lahs-see-coo-roh non eh-rah mee-ah inten-tzee-oh-neh oor-tar-lah.)

No quería darte este empujón.

(Noh kereeyah dárteh ésteh empoohhón.)

Je m'excuse, je vous ai prise pour Elizabeth Taylor.

(Sher mexkiz, sher voozay preez poor _____.)

Scusi, l'avevo presa per Elizabeth Taylor.

(Skoo-zee, lah-veh-voh preh-za per _____.)

Lo siento. Te tomé por Elisabeth Taylor.

(Loh seeyéntoh. Té tohmé pór _____.)

Bonjour, Beauté!

(Bonshoor, Bawtay!)

Ciao, bellezza!

(Chow bel-lets-ah!)

¡Hola, guapa!

(Olah, gwappah!)

ON THE STREET

I'm a talent scout.	Ich bin auf Talentsuche. *(Ish bin aof talent-zooche.)*
I'm an artist; will you pose for me?	Ich bin Maler, würden Sie für mich sitzen? *(Ish bin maaler, vuerden zi fuer mish zitsen?)*
May I come along?	Darf ich Sie begleiten? *(Darf ish zi beglyten?)*
You have such a lovely face.	Sie haben ein unerhört reizvolles Gesicht. *(Zi haaben yn oonairhoert rytsfolles gezisht.)*
I'm lost; can you help me?	Ich habe mich verlaufen; können Sie mir helfen? *(Ish haabe mish ferlaofen; koennen zi mir haylfen?)*
Could you show me the way to _____?	Wie komme ich nach _____? *(Vi komme ish naach _____?)*

FRENCH	ITALIAN	SPANISH
Je suis à la recherche de talents inconnus. *(Sher sweezar la rehshairsh der talan zanconni.)*	È il mio mestiere scoprire nuove stelle. *(Eh eel mee-oh meh-stee-eh-reh sko-pree-reh noo-oh-veh stehl-leh.)*	Soy un hábil explorador. *(Sóy oon ábeel exploradór.)*
Je suis peintre—voulez-vous poser pour moi? *(Sher swee pantr—voolay-voo pozay poor mwar?)*	Sono un artista; mi fa da modella? *(Soh-noh oon artee-stah: mee fah dah model-lah?)*	Soy pintor . . . ?quieres ser mi modelo? *(Sóy peentór . . . keeyéress sér mee modéloh?)*
Puis-je vous accompagner? *(Pweesh voo zacompanyay?)*	Posso accompagnarla? *(Possoh ak-kompah-nee-ar-lah?)*	¿Quieres que te acompañe? *(Keeyéress ké té akom-pányeh?)*
Votre visage est si adorable! *(Votr veezash ay see ador-ahbl!)*	Ha un volto cosí affa-scinante. *(Ah oon voltoh koh-zée af-fah-shee-nan-teh.)*	¡Tienes un rostro tan atractivo . . .! *(Teeyénness oon rróstroh tán atracteeboh . . .!)*
J'ai perdu mon chemin, voulez-vous m'aider? *(Shay perdi mon sherman, voolay-voo maiday?)*	Ho perso la strada; mi può aiutare? *(Oh per-soh lah strah-dah: mee pwo ah-ee-oo-ta-reh?)*	Me he perdido. ¿Podrías ayudarme? *(Meh eh perdeedoh. Pod-reeyass ahyudármeh?)*
S'il vous plaît, pour aller à _____ ? *(Seel voo play, poor allay ar _____ ?)*	Mi può dire la strada per _____ ? *(Mee pwo dee-reh lah strah-dah per _____ ?)*	¿Cómo podría llegar hasta _____ ? *(Kómoh podreeyah llyégar ástah _____ ?)*

ON THE STREET

Didn't we meet in _____ while I was working on my last film?

Haben wir uns nicht während der Produktion meines Filmes in _____ getroffen?

(Haaben vir oons nisht vairend der prodooktion mynes films in _____ ___getroffen?)

I can't remember where I parked my _____.

Jetzt weiss ich nicht mehr, wo ich meinen _____ geparkt habe.

(Yetst vys ish nisht mair, vo ish mynen _____ gepaarkt haabe.)

Please help me; where is the best jeweler in town?

Helfen Sie mir bitte; wo kauft man hier die besten Diamanten?

(Helfen zi mir bitte; vo kaoft man hir di besten di-amaanten?)

Will you show me where I am on this map?

Zeigen Sie mir bitte auf dem Stadtplan, wo ich mich befinde.

(Tsygen zi mir bitte aof dem shtaatplaan, vo ish mish befinde.)

That's very confusing; couldn't you take me there?

Das finde ich nie; können Sie mich nicht begleiten?

(Daas finde ish ni; koennen zi mish nisht beglyten?)

Ne vous ai-je pas vue à _____ pendant que je tournais un film?

(Ner voo zaish par vi ar _____ pandan kersh toornay an feelm?)

Ma non ci siamo incontrati a _____, durante la lavorazione di un mio film?

(Mah non chee see-ah-moh incon-trah-tee ah _____, doo-ran-teh lah lavorah-tzee oh-neh dee oon mee-oh film.)

¿Nos vimos en _____, en la última película que he producido?

(Noss beemoss én_____, én lá oolteemah peleekoolah ké eh prodootheedoh?)

Je ne sais même plus où j'ai laissé ma _____.

(Shern say maim pli oo shay laisay mar _____.)

Non riesco a ricordarmi dove ho posteggiato la mia _____.

(Non ree-eh-skoh ah reecor-dar-mee doh-veh oh pohsteh-jah-toh lah mee-ah _____.)

No puedo recordar dónde he aparcado mi _____ Royce.

(Noh pwéddoh rrecordár dóndeh eh ahparkádoh mee _____.)

Aidez-moi je vous prie: pouvez-vous me montrer la bijouterie où l'on trouve les plus beaux diamants?

(Aiday-mwar, sher voo pree: poovay-voo mer montray la beeshootree oo lon troov lay pli baw dyahman?)

Scusi, ma a _____ dove si comprano i più bei diamanti?

(Skoo-zee, mah ah _____ doh-veh see kom-pranoh ee pew beh-ee dee-ah-mantee?)

Por favor, ¿cuál es el mejor sitio para comprar diamantes en _____?

(Pór fahbór, kwál ess él mehhór seetyoh párah komprár deeyahmántess én _____?)

Pouvez-vous me montrer où nous sommes sur ce plan?

(Poovay-voo mer montray oo noo som sir ser plan?)

Mi può indicare su questa cartina dove mi trovo ora?)

(Mee pwo indicah-reh soo kwestah car-tee-nah doh-ve mee troh-voh oh-rah?)

¿Podrías indicarme dónde estoy, en este mapa?

(Podreeyass eendeekármeh dóndeh stóy, én ésteh mápah?)

C'est vachement compliqué! Pourriez-vous m'accompagner?

(Say vashman compleekay! Pooriay-voo macompanyay?)

Mi pare molto complicato —lei non mi accompagnerebbe?

(Mee pah-reh moltoh complee-cah-toh—leh-ee non mee accompah-nee-eh-rebbeh?)

Es muy complicado, ¿podrías acompañarme?

(Ess mooy kompleekádoh, podreeyass accompanyármeh?)

AT THE RESTAURANT

Is this seat taken?

Ist dieser Platz noch frei?

(Ist diser plaats noch fry?)

Classy hotels are so impersonal; where do you go to meet people?

Elegante Hotels sind so unpersönlich; gibt's hier kein Lokal, wo auch der Mann von der Strasse hingeht?

(Elegante hotels zind zo oonperzoenlish; gibt's hir kyn lokaal, vo aoch der maan fon der shtraase hingayt?)

I'm not very hungry. Are you?

Ich bin nicht sehr hungrig. Du?

(Is bin nisht zair hoongrig. Doo?)

Just one coffee, please, and two straws.

Ober, zwei Strohhalme und einen Kaffee, bitte.

(Ober, tsvy shtro-haalme oond ynen kaaffe, bitte.)

Try some hot peppers.

Wie wär's mit Paprikaschoten/ chinesischem Kompott?

(Vi vair's mit paaprikaa-shoten/ shinayzishem kompott?)

Cette place est prise?

(Set plahs ay preez?)

Questo posto è libero?

(Kwestoh poh-stoh eh leeberoh?)

¿Está ocupada esta silla?

(Stáh okoopádah éstah seellyah?)

Les hôtels chics sont de véritables moulins! Où est-ce qu'on peut rencontrer des gens intéressants?

(Lay zotel sheek son der vaireetabl moolan! Oo eskon per rancontray day shan anterraisan?)

Gli alberghi di lusso sono sempre cosí anonimi; non c'è qualche posto caratteristico dove vanno gli abitanti del luogo?

(Lee albehr-ghee dee loossoh soh-noh sempreh kohzeè anonimee: non chèh kwalkeh poh-stoh carat-tehreestee-koh doh-veh van-noh lee ah-bee-tantee dehl loo-oh-goh?)

En los hoteles elegantes hay demasiado público; ¿no habrá otros lugares más reservados?

(En loss ohtéless ellegántess áy dehmassyádoh poobleekoh; noh abráh otross loogahress máss reserbádos?)

Je n'ai pas très faim. Et vous?

(Sher nay par tray fam. Ay voo?)

Io non ho molta fame. E lei?

(Ee-oh non oh mol-tah fahmeh, eh leh-ee?)

No tengo mucho apetito, ¿y tú?

(Noh téngoh mootchoh appehteetoh, ee too?)

Garçon! Juste un café et deux pailles!

(Garson! Shistan café ay der paee!)

Un caffè solo, cameriere, e due cannucce.

(Oon caf-fèh soh-loh, kahmeh-ree-eh-reh, eh doo-eh kan-noo-cheh.)

Traiga un solo café, camarero, y dos pajas.

(Tráygah oon sóloh kahfé, kahmaréroh, ee dóss páhhass.)

Prenez un peu de piment (Li-chi)

(Prehnay an perd peeman (lee-chee).)

Prenda del caviale/dei nidi di rondine.

(Prehn-dah dehl kah-vee-ah-leh/deh-ee needy dee rondee-neh.)

¿Te gustan los frutos prohibidos?

(Teh goostan loss frootoss proybídoss?)

AT THE RESTAURANT

Since I spilled it on you, let me take you home to change.

Ich habe es verschüttet; darf ich Dich wenigstens nach Haus bringen, damit Du Dich umziehen kannst?

(Ish haabe es fershuettet; daarf ish dish vaynigstens naach haos bringen, damit doo dish oomtsin kaanst?)

ON THE BEACH

Don't move; I'm the lifeguard.

Bitte, nicht rühren—ich bin ein Lebensretter.

(Bitte, nisht rueren—ish bin yn laybensretter.)

I thought you were unconscious so I gave you mouth-to-mouth resuscitation.

Ich dachte, Sie seien ohmächtig, deshalb habe ich Ihnen den Wiederbelebungs-Kuss gegeben.

(Ish dachte, zi zyn ohnmayshtig, deshaalb haabe ish inen dayn viderbelaybungs-kooss gegayben.)

Let me teach you how to swim.

Soll ich Sie Schwimmen lehren?

(Zoll ish zi shwimmen layren?)

FRENCH	ITALIAN	SPANISH
Comme c'est de ma faute que ça s'est renversé sur vos habits, laissez-moi vous accompagner chez vous pour vous changer.	Il minimo che posso fare, dato che sono stato io a versarglielo addosso, è accompagnarla a casa a cambiarsi.	Ya que te he manchado, al menos te llevaré a casa para que te cambies.
(Com sayd mar fawt ker sar say ranvairsay sir vo zabee, laissay-mwar voo zacompanyay shay voo poor voo shanshay.)	*(Eel minimoh keh possoh fah-reh, dah-toh keh sohnoh stah-toh ee-oh ah versarlee-eh-loh addos-so, eh akkom-pah-nee-ar-lah ah kahsah ah kam-bee-ar-see.)*	*(Yah ké teh eh mantcháddoh, ál ménoss teh llyebahré ah kássah párah ké teh kámbyess.)*

Bouge pas; je viens te sauver la vie.	Stia ferma; non vorrei che annegasse.	Quédate quieta; soy el salvavidas.
(Boosh par; sher vyan ter sauvay la vee.)	*(Stee-ah fehrma; non vorray keh an-neh-gas-seh.)*	*(Kédahteh keeyétah; sóy él sahlbábeedass.)*

J'ai cru que tu t'es évanouie, alors je t'ai donné le baiser de vie.	Pensavo che avesse perduto i sensi e allora le ho dato il bacio della vita.	Creí que estabas inconsciente, por esto te hice el boca a boca.
(Shay crik tittay zehvahnwee, alohr shtay donnayl baizay der vee.)	*(Pen-sah-voh keh avehs-seh per-doo-toh ee sensee eh allorah leh oh datoh eel bacho dehl-la veeta.)*	*(Kreh-ee ké stábass eenkonsciénteh, pór ésso teh eethe él bókah ah bókah.)*

Je vais t'apprendre à nager.	Le insegno io a nuotare.	¿Quieres que te enseñe a nadar?
(Sh'vay taprandr ar nashay.)	*(Leh inseh-neeo ee-oh ah noo-oh-tareh.)*	*(Keeyéress ké teh ensénye ah nahdár?)*

ON THE BEACH

Have some of my suntan lotion; I'll rub it on for you.

Nehmen Sie etwas von meinem Sonnenöl; ich reibe es ein.

(Naymen zi etvas fon mynem zonnenoel; ish rybe es yn.)

Were those men bothering you?

Haben diese Männer Sie belästigt?

(Haaben dise maynner zi belay-stigt?)

When does your mother leave?

Wann geht denn Deine Mutter endlich fort?

(Van gayt denn dine mootter ayndlish fort?)

You look cold; let me dry you off.

Sie frieren ja; darf ich Sie abtrocknen?

(Zi friren yaa; darf ish zt abtroknen?)

Let me get the sand off your bathing suit.

Lassen Sie mich den Sand von Ihrem Badeanzug abwischen.

(Lassen zi mish dayn zand fon irem baadeaantsoog abwishen.)

Is this the top of your bikini?

Ist das das Bikini-Oberteil?

(Ist das das bikini obertyl?)

FRENCH	ITALIAN	SPANISH

Prends un peu de mon huile de bronzage; attends, je vais te l'étaler moi-même.

(Pran an pehr d'mon weel der bronzash; attan, shvay ter lettahlay mwar-maim.)

Prenda un po' della mia lozione antisolare; gliela spalmo io.

(Prehn-dah oon poh dehl-la mee-ah loh-tzee-oh-neh anti-soh-la-reh; lee-eh-lah spalmoh ee-oh.)

Toma un poco de loción solar; yo mismo te la pondré.

(Tómah oon pókoh dé lohtheeyón solár; yó meesmoh té lá pondréh.)

Ils t'embêtaient ces gars-là?

(Eel tambaitay say gala?)

Quegli uomini le davano fastidio?

(Kwelly oo-oh-meeny leh dah-vah-noh fastee-deeoh?)

¿Te molestaban estos tipos?

(Teh molesstábahn stos teepos?)

Quand est-ce qu'elle part ta maman?

(Kanteskel parr ta maman?)

Quando se ne va sua madre?

(Kwando seh neh vah soo-ah mah-dreh?)

¿Cuándo se marcha tu mamá?

(Kwándoh sé mártchah too mahmá?)

On dirait que tu as froid; je vais te sécher avec cette serviette.

(On deerayk tair frwar; sher vay tsaichay aveck set serviette.)

Ma lei ha freddo; mi permetta di asciugarla.

(Mah leh-ee ah frehd-doh; mee permet-tah dee ashew-garlah.)

Me parece que tienes frío, voy a secarte con la toalla.

(Mé pahrétheh ké teeyénnes freeyoh, bóy ah sehkárteh kón lah toahllya.)

Attends, je vais enlever le sable de ton maillot de bain.

(Attan, shvay anlervay ler sabl der ton mahyod ban.)

Gliela tolgo io la sabbia dal costume.

(Lee-eh-lah tolgoh ee-oh lah sab-beea dal koh-stoo-meh.)

Déjame que te quite la arena del bañador.

(Déhhameh ké té keeteh lá ahrénah dél bahnyádor.)

C'est le haut de ton bikini, ça?

(Say ler o der ton bikini, sah?)

Questo è parte del suo bikini?

(Kwestoh eh parteh dehl soo-oh bikini?)

¿Esto es la parte superior del bikini?

(Éstoh éss lah párteh sooperiór dél bikini?)

ON THE BEACH

It's the newest kind of artificial respiration.

Das ist die neueste Wiederbelebungstechnik.

(Das ist di noyste viderbelaybungsteshnik.)

I'll hold the towel while you change behind it.

Ich halte das Badetuch und Sie können sich dahinter umziehen.

(Ish halte das badetooch oond zi koennen zish dahinter oomtsin.)

It's the newest kind of artificial respiration.

FRENCH	ITALIAN	SPANISH
Ce que je fais là, c'est la toute dernière méthode de respiration artificielle. *(Ser ker shfay lar, say la toot dairnyair maitod der raispeerasyon arteefeesiel.)*	È il metodo piú moderno di respirazione artificiale. *(Eh eel metodoh pew modern-oh dee reh-spee-rah-tzee-oh-neh artee-fee-cha-leh.)*	Es un nuevo sistema de respiración artificial. *(Ess oon nwévoh systemah dé respirathión artifithiál.)*
Je vais te cacher avec la serviette pendant que tu te changes. *(Shvay tcashay aveck la serviette pandank ti ter shansh.)*	Può cambiarsi dietro l'asciugamano; glielo reggo io. *(Pwò cahm-beear-see dee-eh-troh lashew-gah-manoh; lee-eh-lo reh-go ee-oh.)*	Te aguantaré la toalla mientras te cambias de ropa. *(Té ahgooantahré la tóahllya meeyéntrass té kámbeeyas dé rrópah.)*

31

I'm a masseur; let me loosen up your muscles.

Ich bin Masseur; soll ich Ihre Muskeln auflockern?

(Ish bin maassoer; zoll ish ire moosceln aoflockern?)

The game got me so excited I just had to hug you.

Ich musste Sie in die Arme nehmen, das Spiel hat mich so aufgeregt.

(Ish mooste zi in di arme naymen, das shpil haat mish zo aofgeraygt.)

You'd play better in a shorter skirt.

In einem kürzeren Röckchen würden Sie noch besser spielen.

(In ynem kurtseren roeck-shen vuerden zi noch besser shpilen.)

Let me bandage your knee.

Darf ich Ihr Knie bandagieren?

(Darf ish ir cni baandajiren?)

These packed crowds are so much fun.

So ein Gedränge ist so freundschaftlich.

(Zo yn gedrenge ist zo froynt shaftlish.)

Je suis masseur de profession, je vais vous détendre les muscles.

(Sher swee massehr der professyon, sher vay voo daitandr lay miskl.)

Sono un massaggiatore; lasci che le sciolga i muscoli.

(Soh-noh oon massah-jah-toh-reh; lashee keh leh shohl-gah ee moo-skoh-lee.)

Soy masajista; déjame que te relaje los músculos.

(Sóy massahheestah; déhhah-meh ké teh rreh-láhheh loss mooskooloss.)

Je ne peux pas m'empêcher de vous serrer dans rnes bras, tellement le jeu me fascine!

(Shern per par manpaishay der ´ voo serray dan may brah, tellman ler sher rner faseen!)

È stata l'emozione del gioco —non ho potuto fare a meno di abbracciarla.

(Eh stah-tah leh-moh-tzeeo-neh dehl joh-koh—non oh poh-too-toh fah-reh ah meh-noh dee ab-bra-char-lah.)

No podría hacer lucha contigo; este juego me pone muy nervioso.

(Noh podreeyah athér loot-chah kón-teegoh; ésteh hooéhgoh meh póneh mooy nerbeeyóssoh.)

Vous joueriez tellement mieux en jupe courte!

(Voo shooryay tellman myer an ship coort!)

Se avesse la gonna piú corta giocherebbe meglio.

(Seh ah-vehs-seh lah gohn-nah pew kor-tah joh-keh-reh-beh meh-lee-oh.)

Jugarías mejor con una faldita más corta.

(Hoogahreeyass mehhór kón oonah fahldeetah máss kórtah.)

Je vais vous mettre un bandage autour du genou.

(Sher vay voo metr an bandash awtoor di shernoo.)

Le fascio io il ginocchio.

(Leh fah-shoh ee-oh eel jee-nock-keeoh.)

¿Quieres que te vende la rodilla?

(Keeyéress ké teh béndeh lah rrohdeellyah?)

C'est tellement amusant d'être serrés ainsi dans la foule.

(Say tellman amizan daitr serray ansee dan la fool.)

Questo pigia pigia tra la folla è cosí piacevole.

(Kwestoh pee-jah pee-jah trah lah follah èh ko-zée pee-ah-cheh-voh-leh.)

Estos apretujones entre la multitud resultan muy amistosos.

(Estoss ahprehtoo-hóness éntreh lá moolteetooth ressultan mooy ahmees-tósoss.)

SPORTS

Let me teach you judo.

Ich möchte Ihnen so gerne Jud
beibringen.

(*Ish moeshte inen zo gairn Jud
bybringen.*)

I'll hold you so you won't fall over.

Kommen Sie, ich halte Sie, dam
Sie nicht hinfallen.

(*Kommen zi, ish haalte zi, dam
zi nisht hinfallen.*)

**But the man always does that in figure
skating.**

Das soll aber der Mann bei
akrobatischen Eislaufen mache

(*Daas zoll aaber der maann by
akrobaatishen icelaofen maachen*

AT THE MOVIES

Let's go to a horror film.

Sehen wir uns doch einen Horro
film an.

(*Zayn vir oons doch ynen horro
film an.*)

No, the back row, please.

Nein, bitte die letzte Reihe.

(*Nyn, bitte di laytste ryhe.*)

34

e vais vous apprendre le udo.	Le insegno l'arte del judo.	¿Quieres que te enseñe judo?
Sher vay voo zapprandr er shido.)	*(Le een-seh-nee-oh larteh dehl judoh.)*	*(Keeyéress ké teh ehnsénye hoodoh?)*
e vous tiendrai, comme ça ous ne tomberez pas.	La reggo, cosí non cade.	Te sostendré para que no te caigas.
Sher voo tyandray, com ah voon tombray par.)	*(Lah reh-goh, ko-zée non cah-deh.)*	*(Teh sostendréh párah ké noh teh káygass.)*
Mais le cavalier fait tou-jurs ça dans les figures sur lace!	Ma nelle acrobazie sul ghiaccio l'uomo fa sempre cosí!	En el patinaje artístico, el hombre siempre lo hace así.
May ler cavalyay fay ooshoor sah dan lay feegir r glass!)	*(Mah nehl-leh ah-croh-bah-tzee-eh sool ghee-ah-chee-oh loo-oh-moh fah sehm-preh koh-zée.)*	*(Én él pateenáhheh artís-ticoh, él ómbreh seeyémpreh loh átheh assee.)*
Allons voir un film d'é-ouvante.	Andiamo a vedere un film dell'orrore.	Vamos a ver una película de miedo.
Ahlon vwar an feelm aipoovant.)	*(An-dee-ah-moh ah veh-deh-reh oon film dehl-or-roh-reh.)*	*(Bámos ah bér oonah pehlee-koolah dé meeyédoh.)*
Non, pas ici; la dernière angée s'il vous plaît.	No, nell'ultima fila per favore.	No, la última fila, por favor.
Non, pazeecee; la dairn-air ranshay, seel voo play.)	*(Noh, nehl-ool-tee-mah fee-lah per fah-voh-reh.)*	*(Noh, lah oolteemah feelah, pórr fahbórr.)*

AT THE MOVIES

I'm terribly sorry; I thought it was the armrest.

Tut mir sehr leid, aber ich dach es sei die Armlehne.

(Toot mir zehr lyd, aber ish dach es zy di armlayne.)

Let me remove your coat.

Ich nehme schon ihren Mantel

(Ish nayme shon iren mantel.)

These seats are so narrow I can't move my knee.

Die Sitze sind zu eng, da kann i mein Knie nicht wegnehmen.

(Di zitse zind tsoo ayng, da kan myn cni nisht vaygnaymen.)

I'm sorry my ice cream fell down your dress; let me get it out for you.

O, entschuldigen Sie, jetzt mein Eis in Ihre Bluse gefalle Darf ich es wieder rausnehmen

(O, entshooldigen zi, yetst ist m yce in ire bloose gefallen, darf es vider roasnaymen?)

Je m'excuse, j'ai cru que c'était l'accoudoir. *(Sher mexkiz, shay cri ker setay lakoodwar.)*	Mi scusi tanto, credevo fosse il bracciolo della poltrona. *(Mee scoo-zee tan-toh, creh-deh-voh fos-seh eel brah-cho-loh dehl-la pol-troh-nah.)*	Lo siento mucho, creí que era el brazo de la butaca. *(Loh seeyéntoh mootchoh, kreh-ee ké érah él brátho dé lah boottakah.)*
Laissez-moi vous débarrasser de votre manteau. *(Laisay-mwar voo daibarasay der votr manto.)*	Posso spostare il suo cappotto? *(Pos-soh spoh-stah-reh eel soo-oh cap-pot-toh?)*	Permíteme que te quite la chaqueta. *(Permeeteh-meh ke teh keeteh lah tchakétah.)*
Je ne peux même pas bouger les genoux, ces fauteuils sont si étroits! *(Shern per maim par booshay lay shernoo, say fotey son see aitrwar!)*	Non riesco a muovere il ginocchio, questi sedili sono così stretti. *(Non ree-eh-scoh ah moo-oh-veh-reh eel gee-nok-kee-oh, kwe-stee seh-dee-lee sonoh coh-zeé streht-tee.)*	No puedo mover las rodillas, estos asientos son muy estrechos. *(Noh pwéddoh mohbér lass rrohdeellyas, éstos assyéntos són mooy strétchos.)*
Je m'excuse, ma glace est tombée dans votre col; je vais l'enlever. *(Sher mexkiz, ma glass ay tombay dan votr col; sher vay lanl'vay.)*	Mi dispiace che il mio gelato sia finito nella scollatura del suo abito. Permette che lo riprenda? *(Mee dee-spee-ah-cheh keh eel mee-oh jeh-lah-toh see-ah fee-nee-toh nel-lah skol-la-too-rah dehl soo-oh ah-bee-toh. Per-met-teh keh loh ree-pren-dah?)*	Lo siento, se me ha caido el helado sobre tu vestido. Te lo limpiaré. *(Loh seeyéntoh, seh mé ah kah-eedoh él ehládoh sóbreh too behsteedoh. Teh loh leempyaréh.)*

AT THE ART GALLERY

Please forgive me. Hollander's paintings really turn me on.

Sie müssen mir schon verzeihen aber ich finde Hollande hemmungslos sexy.

(Zi muessen mir shon fertsyn aber ish finde Hollander haym moongslos sexy.)

Are you a model? Nude?

Sind Sie Aktmodell?

(Zind zi aaktmodell?)

Please forgive me. Hollander's paintings really turn me on.

Je vous prie de m'excuser, mais je trouve les tableaux de Hollander terriblement sexy.

(Sher voo pree de mexkizay, may sher troov lay tablaw de Hollander terreeblman sexy.)

Mi perdoni, ma questo artista lo trovo veramente perturbante.

(Mee pehr-dohnee, mah kwehsto artist-ah lo trovo veh-rah-mehnteh per-toor-bahnteh.)

Discúlpame, por favor, pero a Hollander lo encuentro descaradamente sexual.

(Disskoolpah-mah, pórr fahbórr, péroh ah Hollander loh enkwéntroh desskahrádaménteh sekswál.)

Vous êtes modèle? Vous faites du nu?

(Voot zait modell? Voo fait di ni?)

Posa da modella? Nuda?

(Pohsah dah ˘ model-lah? Noo-dah?)

¿Eres modelo? ¿De desnudos?

(Éress mohdéloh? Deh dessnoodoss?)

AT THE ART GALLERY

Please don't move; you look more beautiful than all these pictures.

Bleiben Sir doch bitte 'mal st stehen; Sie sind ja viel schön als alle Gemälde hier.

(Blyben zi doch bitte 'maal sht shtehn; zi zind yaa fiel shoener a alle modelle hier.)

IN YOUR APARTMENT

I'm sorry you can't meet my parents. They had to leave for the weekend.

Schade, dass Du meine Elter nicht treffen kannst. Sie sin plötzlich zum Wochenende for gefahren.

(Shaade, daass doo myne elter nisht treffen kaannst. Zi zir ploetslish tsoon vochenende fortg faaren.)

My etchings are being framed.

Meine Radierungen werde gerahmt.

(Myne raadeeroongen vairde gairahmt.)

It's very lonely here.

Hier ist es sehr einsam.

(Hir ist es zehr ynzam.)

Surtout ne bougez pas, vous êtes tellement plus belle que toutes ces peintures!	La prego, stia ferma. E' piú bella di tutti questi quadri.	No te muevas, por favor. Eres más hermosa que todos estos cuadros.
(Sirtoo ner booshay par, voo zait tellman pli bell ker toot ay pantir.)	*(Lah prego, stee-ah fehrmah. Eh pew beh-lah dee too-tee kwestee kwah-dree.)*	*(Noh teh mwébass, pórr fahbórr. Éress máss ehrmóssah ké tóddoss éstoss kwádross.)*
Je regrette que vous ne puissiez pas voir mes parents, ils sont partis brusquement pour le weekend.	Mi dispiace di non poterti presentare i miei genitori— sono dovuti andar via all'improvviso per il weekend.	Siento que no puedas conocerlos . . . Mis padres han tenido que salir urgentemente de viaje.
(Sher rergret ker voon pweesyay par vwar may paran, el son partee briskerman boor ler week-end.)	*(Mee dees-pee-ah-che dee non po-ter-tee presentah-reh ee mee-eh-ee jeh-nee-tory: soh-noh doh-voo-ty andar vee-ah ahl-limproh-vee-soh per eel weekend.)*	*(Seeyéntoh ké noh pwéddass konothérloss . . . Miss páddres án tehneedoh ké sahleer oorhénteménteh dé beeyáhhe.)*
J'ai donné mes estampes à encadrer.	I quadri che volevo mostrarti sono ancora dal corniciaio.	He llevado todos los cuadros a enmarcar.
(Shay donnay may zestamp ar ancadray.)	*(Ee kwa-dree keh voleh-voh moh-strar-tee soh-noh an-koh-rah dahl kornee-cha-ee-oh.)*	*(Eh llyébádoh tóddos loss kwáddros ah enmaarkár.)*
On est très isolé ici.	Ci si sente molto soli qui.	Se está muy solo aquí.
(Onay tray zeezolay eecee.)	*(Chee see sehn-teh mohl-toh soh-lee kwee.)*	*(Sé stá mooy sóloh akee.)*

IN YOUR APARTMENT

I write music/poetry when I'm lonely.

Ich dichte/komponiere, um di Einsamkeit zu verjagen.

(Ish dishte/komponire, oom ynzamkyt tsoo feryaagen.)

Let me take your coat.

Komm, gib' mir Deinen Mante

(Komm gib' mir dynen maantel.

That's embroidery on your blouse, isn't it?

Ist das Stickerei da an Deine Bluse?

(Ist daas shtikery daa an dyn bloose?)

Make yourself comfortable; take your shoes off.

Zieh' Deine Schuhe aus, das i viel bequemer.

(Tsi dyne shoo aos, daas ist j bequemer.)

If you're too warm, why don't you take off your sweater?

Ich habe die Heizung gern Volldampf, zieh' Deinen Pu Deine Strickjacke aus, wen Dir zu warm ist.

(Ish habe di hytsoong gern folldaamf; tsi dynen pully/d shtrikyacke aos, ven's dir t vaarm ist.)

FRENCH	ITALIAN	SPANISH

e fais de la musique j'écris des poèmes) pour ublier ma solitude.

Sher' fay dlar mizeek shaykree day po-aim) poor obleeay ma soleetid.)

Per riempire la mia solitudine scrivo musica/poesia.

(Per ree-ehm-pee-reh lah mee-ah solitoo-dee-neh skree-voh moo-see-kah/ poh-eh-zee-ah.)

Escribo música/poesías para distraer mi soledad.

(Screeboh moosicah/poesíass párah distraér mee soledád.)

---

aissez-moi vous débarrasser de votre manteau.

Laissay-mwar voo daiba-assay der votr manto.)

Si vuol togliere il cappotto?

(See voo-ohl toh-lee-eh-reh eel kap-pot-toh?)

Deja que te quite la chaqueta.

(Déhha ké té keeteh lá tchakétah.)

'est de la broderie ce que ous avez là sur votre hemisier?

Say dlar brodree ser ker oo zavay lar sir votr hemeezyay?)

Quelli lí sono ricami sulla sua camicetta?

(Kwel-lée-lee soh-noh ree-kah-mee sool-lah soo-ah kamee-chet-tah?)

¿Este bordado es de tu blusa?

(Esteh bordádoh ess dé too bloosah?)

Débarrassez-vous de vos haussures, vous serez plus l'aise!

Daibarassay-vood vo shaw-sir, voo sray plizalaiz!)

Si tolga le scarpe; starà piú comoda.

(See tohl-gah leh scar-peh; stah-rah pew ko-moh-dah.)

Quítate los zapatos, estarás más cómoda.

(Kíttateh loss thahpátoss, staráss máss kómohdah.)

J'aime bien que le chauffage soit à fond, mais si vous avez trop chaud n'hésitez pas à tomber le cardigan (le pull).

(Shaim byan kler shawfash swatar fon, may see voo zavày tro shaw naizeetay pazar tombay ler cardeegan (ler pil).)

A me piace la casa ben riscaldata ma se lei ha troppo caldo si tolga pure il golf.

(Ah meh pee-ah-che lah ka-zah ben rees-kal-dah-tah mah seh leh-ee ah trop-poh kal-doh see tohl-gah poo-reh eel golf.)

Me gusta la calefacción a toda marcha, pero puedes quitarte la chaqueta/el jersey, si tienes calor.

(Meh goostah lá calefakthión ah tóddah márchah, péroh pwéddes kittárteh lá tchakétah/él herséy, see teeyénnes kahlór.)

43

IN YOUR APARTMENT

Can I get you a cocktail instead?

Nimm doch lieber einen Cocktail

(Nimm doch liber ynen cocktail.)

I'm so excited that this cocktail is shaking itself.

Ich mixe nicht—das ist Aufre gung.

(Ish mixe nisht—daas ist aofray goong.)

Come see the view from the bedroom window.

Die schönste Aussicht hat man von dem Fenster hier am Bett.

(Di shoenst aosisht hat maan for dem fenster hir aam bett.)

I can't cook; I live on sandwiches.

Kochen kann ich nicht; ich ess immer nur Schnitten.

(Kochen kaann ish nisht; ish ayss imer noor shnitten.)

Essayez plutôt un cocktail. *(Essaiyay plito an cock-ail.)*	Provi un po' questo cocktail che ho inventato io. *(Proh-vee oon poh kwestoh cocktail keh oh inven-tah-toh ee-oh.)*	Será mejor que tomes un combinado. *(Seráh mehhór ké tómess oon kombeenádoh.)*
Je n'ai pas de shaker; mais e garantis le mélange! *(Sher nay pard shaikair; nay sher garanteel mai-lansh!)*	No, non sto agitando il cocktail; sono semplicemente eccitato. *(Noh, non stoh ah-jee-tandoh eel cocktail; soh-noh sehm-plee-che-men-teh etch-chee-tah-toh.)*	No tengo coctelera; resulta muy excitante. *(Noh téngoh cocktelérah; resultah mooy exceetánteh.)*
Viens voir la belle vue qu'on a du lit à travers la fenêtre. *(Vyan vwahr la bell vi konar di lee a travair la fernaitr.)*	Venga a vedere il panorama da questa finestra vicino al letto. *(Vengah ah veh-deh-reh eel panorama dah kwestah fee-neh-strah vee-chee-noh ahl let-toh.)*	Ven a mirar el paisaje desde esta ventana junto a la cama. *(Bén ah meerár él payssáhhe désdeh éstah bentánah huntoh ah lá kámah.)*
Je ne sais pas faire la cuisine; je me nourris de sandwiches. *(Shern say par fair la cweezeen; sherm nooree de sandweech.)*	Io non so cucinare; vivo di panini. *(Ee-oh non soh coo-chee-nareh; vee-voh dee pah-nee-nee.)*	No sé cocinar; vivo de bocadillos. *(Noh sé cotheenár; beeboh dé bokadeellyoss.)*

IN YOUR APARTMENT

We blew a fuse.

Jetzt ist Kurzschluss.

(Yetst ist courts-shlooss.)

Let's dance in the bedroom; that's
where I keep my stereo.

Tanzen wir doch im Schla
zimmer, da ist das Radio.

*(Tantsen vir doch im shlaaf
simmer, daa ist daas raadio.)*

FRENCH	ITALIAN	SPANISH
Les plombs ont sauté.	È saltata una valvola.	Se han fundido los plomos.
(Lay plon on sautay.)	*(Eh sal-tah-tah oo-nah val-voh-lah.)*	*(Sé án foondíddoh loss plómoss.)*
Viens danser dans ma chambre, c'est là que je mets la radio.	Vieni a ballare in camera da letto, dove ho la radio.	Vamos a bailar al dormitorio, donde tengo la radio.
(Vayn dansay dan ma shambr, say lark sher may lar rahdio.)	*(Vee-eh-ny ah bal-lah-reh een camerah dah let-toh, do-veh oh lah rah-deeoh.)*	*(Bámoss ah baylár ál dormeettórioh, dóndeh téngoh lá rádioh.)*

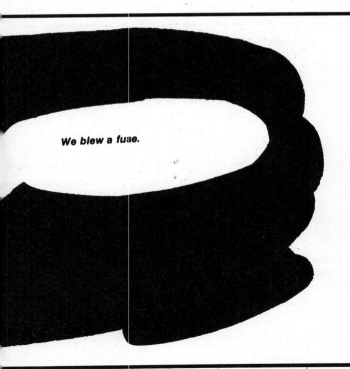

We blew a fuse.

IN YOUR APARTMENT

I'm sorry, I can't get the door unlocked.

Tut mir leid, das Türschlos klemmt.

(Toot mir lyd, daas tuershlos klemmt.)

I didn't realize the clock had stopped.

Hab' gar nicht bemerkt, dass die Uhr stehengeblieben ist.

(Haab' gar nisht bemayrkt, daas di oor shtehen gebliben ist.)

The taxis stopped running an hour ago.

Taxis fahren schon seit einer Stunde nicht mehr.

(Taxis faaren shon zyt yner shtoonde nisht mair.)

Nobody will ever know.

Merkt doch kein Mensch.

(Mairkt doch kyn mensh.)

Why not take a bath? I won't look.

Willst Du nicht baden? Ich gucke nicht.

(Villst doo nisht baaden? Ish gooke nisht.)

I'm afraid the bathroom door won't lock.

Die Badezimmertür schliesst leider nicht.

(Di baadetsimmer-tuer shlihst lyder nisht.)

FRENCH	ITALIAN	SPANISH
Zut alors! le verrou est coincé!	Mi spiace, ma si è bloccata la serratura.	Lo siento, la cerradura se ha atascado.
(Zit alor! ler vairoo ay kwansay!)	*(Mee spee-ah-che, mah see eh block-kah-tah lah seh-rah-too-rah.)*	*(Loh seeyéntoh, lah thérrah-doorah sé ah atasskádoh.)*
Je ne me suis même pas aperçu que le réveil s'est arrêté.	Non mi ero accorto che s'era fermato l'orologio.	No me había dado cuenta de que el reloj estaba parado.
(Shern mer swee maim par zapairsi kerl raivay set arettay.)	*(Non mee eh-roh ak-kor-toh keh seh-rah fer-mah-toh loh-roh-loh-jee-oh.)*	*(Noh mé abbíah dádoh kwéntah dé ké él rrelóhh stábah pahrádoh.)*
Ça fait une heure que les taxis ont cessé de circuler.	Non ci sono più tassí a quest'ora.	Los taxis ya no circulan desde hace una hora.
(Sar fay in ehr ker lay taxee on cessay dseerkilay.)	*(Non chee soh-noh pew tas-sée ah kwestoh-rah.)*	*(Loss táxis yah nó thirkoolan désdeh átheh oonah órah.)*
Personne ne le saura.	Non lo saprà nessuno.	Nadie lo sabrá.
(Pairsonn ner ler sawrah.)	*(Non loh sah-pràh nes-soo-noh.)*	*(Náddye loh sabráh.)*
Tu peux prendre un bain, tu sais . . . Je ne regarderai pas!	Fa un bagno. Io non guardo.	¿Por qué no te bañas? No miraré.
(Ti per prandr an ban, ti say . . . Shern rehgardray par!)	*(Fah oon bah-nee-oh. Ee-oh non goo-ar-doh.)*	*(Pór ké nó teh bányass? Nó meerah-réh.)*
J'ai bien peur qu'on ne puisse pas fermer à clé la porte de la salle de bain.	Mi dispiace, ma la porta del bagno non si chiude.	Lamento mucho que la puerta del baño no cierre.
(Shay byan pehr koon pwees par fairmay ar clay la port der la sal der ban.)	*(Mee deespee-ah-cheh, mah lah portah dehl bah-nee-oh non see kew-deh.)*	*(Laméntoh mootchoh ké lá pwértah dél bányo nó theey-érreh.)*

IN HER APARTMENT

It's rather warm; may I take my jacket off?

Es ist recht warm hier, darf ich meine Jacke ausziehen?

(Es ist raycht vaarm hir, daarf ish myne yaacke oastsihen?)

I bought a bottle of something unusual for a change.

Ich habe heute zur Abwechslung ein ganz besonderes Fläschchen gekauft.

(Ish haabe hoyte tsoor abvayxloong yn gaans bezondres flaysh-shen gekaoft.)

Where is the bedroom?

Wo ist das Schlafzimmer?

(Vo ist daas schlaaftsimmer?)

I'm tired; may I lie down?

Ich bin müde—darf ich mich ein Weilchen hinlegen?

(Ish bin muede—darf ish mish yn vylshen hinlaygen?)

Why don't you lie down, too? You look a bit tired.

Leg' Dich doch auch ein Weilchen hin, Du siehst auch müde aus.

(Layg' dish doch aoch yn vylshen hin, doo zïst aoch muede aos.)

FRENCH	ITALIAN	SPANISH
Il fait un peu chaud; vous permettez que je tombe la veste?	Fa piuttosto caldo, posso togliermi la giacca?	Hace calor, ¿ puedo quitarme la americana?
(Eel faitan per shaw; voo pairmetay ker sher tomb la vest?)	(Fah pewt-toh-stoh kal-doh, pos-soh toh-lee-ehr-mee lah jah-kah?)	(Athe kahlór, pwéddo kittármeh lá americánah?)
J'ai apporté une petite bouteille qui est pas piquée des hannetons.	Tanto per cambiare ho comprato una bottiglia di qualcosa di insolito.	Compré una botella de algo raro, para variar.
(Shay apportay in pteet bootay kee nay par peekay day anton.)	(Tahn-toh per cahm-bee-ah-reh oh kom-prah-toh oonah bot-tee-lee-ah dee kwal-ko-sah dee een-soh-lee-toh.)	(Kompré oonah bottehllya dé álgoh rároh, párah bareeyár.)
Où est la chambre à coucher?	Dov'è la camera da letto?	¿Dónde está el dormitorio?
(Oo ay la shambr ar cooshay?)	(Doh-vèh lah camerah dah let-toh?)	(Dóndeh stá él dormeettórioh?)
Je me sens un peu fatigué; est-ce que je peux m'étendre un moment?	Sono stanco, posso sdraiarmi?	Estoy cansado, ¿puedo estirarme un rato?
(Sherm san an per fateegay; esker sher per maitandr an moman?)	(Soh-no stahn-koh, pos-soh sdrah-eearmee?)	(Stóy kansádoh, pwéddoh steerármeh oon rátoh?)
Viens un peu près de moi! Tu as l'air fatiguée.	Perché non ti sdrai anche tu? Mi sembri un po' stanca.	¿Por qué no te acuestas tu también? Pareces un poco cansada.
(Vyan an per pray der mwar! Ti ar lair fateegay.)	(Per-kéh non tee sdrah-ee an-keh too? Mee sehm-bree oon poh stahn-kah.)	(Pór ké noh té akwéstass too tambeeyén? Paréthess oon pókoh cansádah.)

51

IN HER APARTMENT

There's a lovely view from this couch.

Schöne Aussicht hat man von hier.

(Shoene aosisht hat maan for hir.)

I think I'm going to faint.

Jetzt werde ich ohnmächtig.

(Jaytst verde ish ohnmayshtig.)

What lovely, smooth hands you have. Put them here.

Was für schöne weiche Hände Du hast; leg' sie hier hin.

(Vaas fuer shoene vyshe haynde doo hast; layg zi hir hin.)

I feel unworthy of anyone as lovely as you.

So etwas Süsses wie Du bist habe ich nicht verdient.

(Zo etvas zuesses vi doo bist haabe ish nisht ferdihnt.)

When does your husband get back?

Wann kommt Dein Mann nach Hause?

(Van kommt dyn mann nach haose?)

I'm here to read the electric meter.

Ich habe nur die elektrische Zähluhr abgelesen.

(Ish haabe noor di elektrishe tsayloor abgelayzen.)

FRENCH	ITALIAN	SPANISH
On a une de ces vues, de ce sofa!	C'è una vista stupenda da questo divano.	Se ve una vista preciosa desde esta cama.
(Onar in der say vi, der ser sofar.)	*(Cheh oo-nah vee-stah stoo-pen-dah dah kwestoh dee-vah-noh.)*	*Sé bé oonah beestah pre-theeósah désdeh éstah kámah.)*
Je me sens mal.	Mi sento svenire.	Me siento desfallecido.
(Sherm san mal.)	*(Mee sen-toh sveh-nee-reh.)*	*(Mé seeyéntoh desfahlly-ethído.)*
Ce que tu as de belles mains...! mets-les là!	Che belle manine morbide, mettile qui.	¡Qué manos tan suaves tienes! ¡Pónlas ahí!
(Sker ti ar der bell man...! may-lay lar!)	*(Keh bel-leh mah-nee-neh mor-bee-deh, met-tee-leh kwee.)*	*(Ke mánoss tán swábes teeyénnes! Pónlass ah-ee.)*
Je me sens indigne d'une belle fille comme toi (vous).	Non sono degno di una deliziosa creatura come te.	Me siento indigno de una mujer tan encantadora como tú.
(Sherm san andeen din bell feey com twar (voo).)	*(Non soh-noh deh-neeo dee oo-nah deh-lee-tzee-oh-zah creh-ah-too-rah koh-meh teh.)*	*(Meh seeyéntoh indígnoh deh oonah moohhér tán enkantahdórah kómoh too.)*
Quand est-ce qu'il rentre, ton mari?	A che ora torna tuo marito?	¿A qué hora vuelve tu marido?
(Kanteskeel rantr, ton maree?)	*(Ah keh oh-rah tor-nah too-oh mah-ree-toh?)*	*(Ah ké órah bwélbe too mahríddoh?)*
Je suis venu relever le compteur électrique.	Sono venuto a leggere il contatore dell'elettricità.	He venido a leer el contador de la electricidad.
(Sher swee verni rehlvay ler contehr ellektreek.)	*(Soh-noh veh-noo-toh ah ledge-eh-reh eel kon-tah-toh-reh dehl eh-leh-tree-chee-tàh.)*	*(Eh behneedoh ah leh-ér él kontahdór dé lá electrithi-dád.)*

STUCK IN THE ELEVATOR

The alarm bell doesn't work.

Der Alarm funktioniert nicht.

(Der alaarm fooktionirt nisht.)

We'll probably be here for hours.

Wir werden hier wohl stundenlang festsitzen.

(Vir verden hir vohl shtoonden laang festzitsen.)

I know a little game to pass the time.

Sollen wir uns mit einem kleinen Spiel die Zeit vertreiben?

(Zollen vir oons mit ynem klynen shpil di tsit fertryben?)

Lean on me if you like.

Lehnen Sie sich an mich.

(Laynen zi zish aan mish.)

FRENCH	ITALIAN	SPANISH

La sonnette d'alarme ne marche pas.

(La saunet dalarm ner marsh par.)

Il campanello d'allarme non funziona.

(Eel kahm - pah - nehl - loh dahl-lar-meh non foon-tzee-oh-nah.)

El timbre de alarma no funciona.

(El teembreh dé ahlármah noh foonthiyónah.)

On va être coincés ici pendant des heures.

(On va aitr kwansay eecee pandan day zehr.)

Probabilmente resteremo qui per delle ore.

(Probah-beel-mehn-teh rest-eh-reh-moh kwee per dehl-leh oh-reh.)

Seguramente pasaremos aquí varias horas.

(Sehgoorahménteh pahsarémos ahkee báreeyas óras.)

Je connais un petit jeu pour passer le temps.

(Sher connay an ptee sher poor passayl tan.)

So un bel giuoco per passare il tempo.

(Soh oon behl joh-koh per pass-ah-reh eel tempoh.)

Conozco un lindo juego para pasar el rato.

(Kohnóthkoh oon leendoh hooégho párah passár él rrátoh.)

Appuie-toi sur moi, si tu veux.

(Apwee-twar sir mwar, see ti ver.)

Si appoggi pure a me.

(See ahp-poh-jee poo-reh ah meh.)

Apóyate en mí, si quieres.

(Appóyahteh én mee, see keeyéress.)

IN THE HOTEL

Mr. and Mrs. Smith.

Herr und Frau Schmidt.
(Herr oond frao shmitt.)

A room with a double bed.

Bitte ein Zimmer mit Doppelbett.
(Bitte, yn tsimmer mit doppel-bett.)

One lump or two, dear?

Nimmst Du ein oder zwei Stück-chen Zucker?

(Nimmst doo yn oder tsy shtueck-shen tsoocker?)

Of course we're married!

Natürlich sind wir verheiratet!
(Natuerlish zind vir ferhyraatet!)

How dare you!

Was fällt Ihnen ein!
(Vaas faylt ihnen yn?)

But I thought they were real ones!

Ich dachte, die sind echt.
(Ish daachte, di zind aysht.)

Monsieur et Madame Smith.	Il signore e la signora Smith.	El señor y la señora Smith.
(Mersyer ay Madahm Smith.)	*(Eel see-nyo-reh eh lah see-nyo-rah Smith.)*	*(El sehnyórr ee lah sehn-yórah Smith.)*
Une chambre avec un lit à deux places.	Una camera matrimoniale.	Una habitación con cama de matrimonio.
(In shambr aveck an lee ar der plahs.)	*(Oona camera mah-tree-mo-nee-aleh.)*	*(Oonah abeetahthión kón kámah deh matrimónioh.)*
Un óu deux morceaux, mon chou?	Una o due zollette, cara?	¿Un terrón o dos, querida?
(Anoo der morsaw, mon shoo?)	*(Oona oh dweh tzoh-leh-teh, cah-rah?)*	*(Oon tehrrón oh dóss, keh-reedah?)*
Quelle question! Bien sûr que nous sommes mariés!	Certo che siamo sposati!	¡Claro que estamos casados!
(Kel kestyon!) Byan sir ker noo somm mariay!)	*(Chair-to keh sya-moh spoh-sahtee!)*	*(Clároh ké stámmoss kahs-sádoss!)*
Quelle insolence!	Come osa?	¿Cómo se atreve?
(Kel ansolans!)	*(Koh-meh oh-sah?)*	*(Kómoh seh ahtrébeh?)*
Et moi qui croyais qu'ils étaient vrais!	Ma io credevo che fossero veri.	¡Creí que eran de verdad!
(Ay mwar kee crwahyay keel zettay vray!)	*(Mah yo creh-deh-vo keh foh-seh-ro veh-ree.)*	*(Kreh-ee ké érahn deh behr-dád.)*

IN THE HOTEL

Do you snore?

Schnarchst Du?
(*Shnarsh-st doo?*)

Fantastic!

Toll!
(*Toll!*)

You'll ruin the creases.

Gib' auf meine Bügelfalten acht.
(*Gib' aof myne buegelfaalten aacht.*)

What cold feet you have.

Du hast ja so kalte Füsse.
(*Doo hast yaa zo kaalte fuesse.*)

That tickles.

Das kitzelt.
(*Das kitselt.*)

How did it get like that?

Wie kommt das?
(*Vi kommt das?*)

Undo this, please.

Mach' das bitte 'mal auf.
(*Maach das bitte 'maal aof.*)

It's stuck.

Es geht nicht auf.
(*Es gayt nisht aof.*)

FRENCH	ITALIAN	SPANISH
Tu ronfles? (*Ti ronfl?*)	Tu russi? (*Too roo-ssee?*)	¿Roncas? (*Rónkass?*)
Fantastique! (*Fantasteek!*)	Fantastico! (*Fantastic-o!*)	¡Fantástico! (*Fantásticoh!*)
Tu vas m'esquinter le pli. (*Ti var meskantay ler plee.*)	Sciuperai la piega. (*Shoo-per-ah-ee lah pee-eh-gah.*)	Estropearás los pliegues. (*Strohpeh-ahráss loss pleeyeghess.*)
Oh, ce que tu as les pieds glacés! (*Oh, sker ti ar lay pyay glahsay!*)	Che piedi freddi hai! (*Keh pee-eh-dee freh-dee ah-ee!*)	¡Qué pies tan fríos tienes! (*Ké peeyéss tán freeyoss teeyénness!*)
Ça chatouille. (*Sah shatooy.*)	Mi fa il solletico. (*Mee fah eel sol-leh-tee-ko.*)	Hace cosquillas. (*Átheh koskeellyass.*)
Comment ça se fait? (*Comman sass fay?*)	Come hai fatto? (*Coh-meh ah-ee fah-toh?*)	¿Cómo me he puesto así? (*Kómoh meh eh pwéstoh assee?*)
Défais ca, tu veux? (*Deffay sah, ti ver?*)	Aprimi questo, per favore. (*Ah-pree-mee kweh-sto per fah-voreh.*)	Quítate eso, ¿quieres? (*Kittah-teh éssoh, keeyéress?*)
C'est coincé! (*Say kwansay!*)	Non si apre. (*Non see ah-preh.*)	Está muy apretado. (*Stáh mooy ahprehtádoh.*)

I don't think he believes us.

Dieser Kerl glaubt uns doch nicht.

(Dizer kairl glaobt oons doch nisht.)

Try to look natural.

Benimm Dich ganz natürlich.

(Benimm dish gaans naatuerlish.)

Not so close to the window.

Nicht so nah am Fenster.

(Nisht zo naa aam fenster.)

Try to look natural.

Je ne crois pas qu'il nous ait crus.

(Shern crwah par keel noo zay cri.)

Penso che non ci creda.

(Pen-soh keh non chee creh-dah.)

Supongo que no nos han creido.

(Sooppóngoh ké noh noss ahn kreh-eedoh.)

Prends un air naturel.

(Pran anair natirell.)

Cerca di essere naturale.

(Chair-kah dee eh-seh-reh nah-too-rahleh.)

Trata de aparecer natural.

(Trátah deh ahpahrehther natoorál.)

Ne t'approche pas trop de la fenêtre!

(Ner taprosh par tro der la fernaitr.)

Non cosí vicino alla finestra.

(Non ko-seé vee-chee-no al-lah fee-nest-rah.)

No tan cerca de la ventana.

(Noh tán zehrkah deh lah behntánah.)

IN THE HOTEL

Is this the first time for you?

Das erstemal?

(Das airstemaal?)

Why not?

Warum nicht?

(Varoom nisht?)

Don't worry; I've already had the mumps.

Das macht nichts; ich hatte voriges Jahr Ziegenpeter.

(Das maacht nishts; ish hatte foriges Jaar tsigenpeter.)

I have a book that shows all kinds of ways to do it—and the good pages are marked.

Ich habe hier ein Buch mit verschiedenen Tips. Die Seiten sind markiert.

(Ish haabe hier yn booch mit fershidenen tips; di zyten zind markiert.)

You mean *you* wrote it?

Hast Du es geschrieben?

(Hast doo es geshriben?)

FRENCH	ITALIAN	SPANISH
C'est la première fois...? *(Say la prermyair fwar...?)*	É la prima volta? *(Eh lah pree-mah volt-ah?)*	¿Es la primera vez? *(Ess lah preeméhrah béth?)*
Pourquoi pas? *(Poorkwar par?)*	Perché no? *(Per-keh no?)*	¿Por qué no? *(Pór ké noh?)*
Y a pas de danger, j'ai eu les oreillons l'année dernière! *(Yah pard danshay, shay i lay zorayon lannay dernyair!)*	Non aver paura—ho avuto gli orecchioni l'anno scorso. *(Non ah-vehr pah-oo-ra, oh ah-vooto lee oh-reh-kioh-nee l'ahno scor-so.)*	Todo irá bien. Tuve las paperas el año pasado. *(Tóddoh eeráh beeyén. Toobeh lass pahpérass él ányoh passádoh.)*
J'ai un livre qui indique toutes les positions; jette un coup d'œil, j'ai marqué les pages. *(Shay an leevr kee andeek toot lay pozeesyon; shett an koo dei, shay markay lay pash.)*	Ho un manuale che insegna metodi diversi: le pagine sono segnate. *(Oh oon mah-noo-ah-leh keh in-seh-nyaa meh-to-dee divers-ee; leh pa-jee-neh sono se-nya-teh.)*	Tengo un libro que lo explica de varias formas; las páginas están señaladas. *(Téngoh oon leebroh ké loh expleekah deh báreeyas fórmass; lass páhhenass stán sehnyaládass.)*
C'est toi qui a écrit ça? *(Say twar kee ar aikree sah?)*	L'hai scritto tu? *(Lah-ee scree-toh too?)*	¿Lo escribiste tu? *(Loh screebeesteh too?)*

I'm a news photographer; may I take your picture?

Ich bin Pressefotograf; darf ich von Ihnen eine Aufnahme machen?

(Ish bin presse-fotograaf, daarf is fon ihnen yne aofnaame maachen?

Just lift your skirt a bit so I can get a shot of those lovely legs.

Den Rock ein bisschen höher bitte, damit Ihre schönen Beine ganz auf's Bild kommen.

(Den rock yn biss-shen hoeher bitte, daamit ihre shoenen byn gans aof's bild kommen.)

Actually I work for_____magazine; how about a picture?

Ich arbeite ja eigentlich für _____; wie wär's mit eine Aufnahme für die Zeitschrift?

(Ish arbyte yaa ygentlish fu _____; vi vair's mit yner aoj naame fuer di tsytshrift?)

I prefer nude photography because the texture of female flesh is so expressive.

Am liebsten mache ich Aktaul nahmen, weil die weibliche Hau so ausdrucksvoll ist.

(Am liebsten maache ish aaki aofnaamen, vyl di vyblishe haot z aosdrooks-foll ist.)

FRENCH	ITALIAN	SPANISH
Je suis reporter photographe, je peux vous prendre une photo? *(Sher swee rehportair-photograff, sher per voo prandr in photaw?)*	Sono un foto-reporter. Posso fotografarla? *(Sono oon foto-reporter. Posoh photo-gra-pharlah?)*	Soy fotógrafo de prensa, ¿puedo sacarte una fotografía? *(Sóy photógrahfoh deh prénsah, pwéddoh sahkárrteh oonah photographyah?)*
Soulevez un peu la jupe que je puisse photographier ces belles jambes que vous avez! *(Soolvay an per la ship kersh pweece photografyay say bell shamb ker voo zavay!)*	Alzi un po' la gonna; vorrei mettere in risalto le sue meravigliose gambe. *(Ahltzee oon poh lah gohnah; voray meh-tehreh in ree-sahl-to leh sweh mehrahvee-lyoseh gahm-beh.)*	Levántate un poquito la falda para que pueda retratar tus bonitas piernas. *(Lebántah-teh oon pokeetoh lah fáldah párah ké pwéddah rehtrah-tárr toos boneetass peeyernass.)*
En réalité, je travaille pour _____; ça vous dirait de poser pour ce magazine? *(An raiahleetay, sher travaee poor _____; sah voo deeray der pozay poor ser magazeen?)*	Lavoro per la rivista_____ ___—vorrei pubblicare una sua fotografia. *(Lah-voro per lah ree-veesta _____ — voray poobleekah-reh oona swah photograph-ya.)*	En realidad trabajo para _____, ¿qué te parece que te haga unas fotos para esta revista? *(En reh-ahleedád trahbáhhoh párah _____, ké te parétheh ké teh ágah oonass phótoss párah éstah rehbeestah?)*
Je préfère faire des nus, car les femmes ont une texture de peau si expressive! *(Sher preffair day ni, kahr lay famm ontin textir der paw see expresseev!)*	Preferisco i nudi. Trovo la pelle femminile così fotogenica! *(Prefer-eeskoh ee noo-dee. Trovo lah peh-leh feh-meeneeleh kosèe photogenic-ah.)*	Prefiero la fotografía de desnudo porque la textura de la carne femenina es tan expresiva . . . *(Prehfeeyéroh lah photographyah deh dessnoodoh pór-ké lah textoorah deh lah kárneh fehmehneenah ess tán expressibah . . .)*

TAKING PICTURES

My studio is in my apartment.

Das Atelier ist in meine Wohnung.

(Das aatelyeh ist in myne vonoong.)

This is a special camera. It doesn't need film.

Das ist eine besondere Kamera die braucht keinen Film.

(Das ist yne bezondere camera, a braocht kynen film.)

Don't be shy; think of me as a doctor.

Nicht so schüchtern; stell' Di vor, ich bin Dein Arzt.

(Nisht zo shuesh-tern; shtell d for ish bin dyn aartst.)

AT HER PARENTS' HOME

You must be her sister, not her mother!

Sie sind doch bestimmt di Schwester, nicht die Mutter!

(Zi zind doch beshtimmt di shves ter, nisht di mootter!)

What magnificent cooking!

Das schmeckt ja grossartig!

(Daass shmeckt yaa grossaartig!)

Mon appartement me sert e studio. *Mon apparterman mer sair r stidyaw.)*	Ho lo studio nel mio appartamento. *(Oh lo stoo-dio nehl mee-o ahpart-ahmento.)*	Tengo el estudio en mi piso. *(Téngoh el stood-yoh en mee peesoh.)*
'est un appareil photo récial qui n'a pas besoin e film. *Settan apparay photaw aisyal kee nah par berzand feelm.)*	Questa è una macchina speciale: non ha bisogno di pellicola. *(Kwehstah eh oona makeenah speh-chah-leh. Non ah bee-sonyo dee pehlleekolah.)*	Es una cámara especial, que no necesita película. *(Ess oonah cámahrah spethiál, ké noh nethessíttah pehl-leekoolah.)*
e soyez pas intimidée, ites comme si j'étais votre octeur. *Ner swayay par zanteeeeday, fait comm see ettay votr doctehr.)*	Non sia così timida. Faccia conto che io sia un medico. *(Non see-ah kosèe timid-ah. Fah-chah con-to keh yo see-ah oon meh-dee-ko.)*	No tengas vergüenza, piensa en mí como médico. *(Noh téngass behrg-wénthah, peeyénsah én mee kómoh médeekoh.)*
suis sûr que vous êtes sa eur; pas sa mère, c'est ipossible! *Sher swee sir ker voo zait sehr; par sa mair, settam ossible!)*	Ma lei è la sorella, non la mamma! *(Mah leh-ee eh lah sohrehl-lah, non lah mammah!)*	¡Usted debe de ser su hermana, y no su madre! *(Oostéd débeh deh sérr soo ehrmánah, ee noh soo máddreh!)*
ous êtes un véritable rdon bleu! *'oo zait an vaireetabl rdon blehr!)*	Che magnifico pranzo! *(Keh mah - nee - fee - koh prahn-tzoh!)*	¡Qué comida más exquisita! *(Ké kohmeedah máss exkeeseetah!)*

67

AT HER PARENT'S HOME

I don't make very much money.

Ich verdiene noch sehr wenig.

(Ish ferdine noch zehr venig.)

I'm just a student.

Ich bin ja nur Student.

(Ish bin yaa noor shtoodend.)

This is a great dish. May I have some more?

Darf ich noch etwas von dies köstlichen Speise haben?

(Daarf ish noch etvaas von diz koestlishen shpyze haaben?)

I hope one day I may be worthy of your daughter.

Ich hoffe, ich werde Ihrer Tocl ter eines Tages wert sein.

(Ish hoffe, ish verde irer tocht ynes taages vert zyn.)

When exactly will you be away and for how long?

Wann fahren Sie fort? Auf w lange?

(Van faahren zi fort? aof laange?)

I'm afraid I couldn't marry her; my wife would object.

Heiraten kann ich Ihre Tochte nicht; meine Frau würde en schieden dagegen sein.

(Hiraaten kaann ish ire tochte nisht; myne frao vuerde entshide dagegen zyn.)

FRENCH	ITALIAN	SPANISH
Mon salaire est ridicule.	Guadagno assai poco.	Gano muy poco
(Mon sahlair ay reedeekil.)	*(Gwah-dah-nee-oh ahs-sah-ee poh-koh.)*	*(Gáhnoh mooy pókoh.)*
Je ne suis qu'un étudiant.	Sono ancora studente.	Sólo soy un estudiante.
(Shern swee kan aitidyan.)	*(Soh-noh ahn-ko-rah stoo-den-teh.)*	*(Sóloh sóy oon stoodeeyán-teh.)*
Puis-je me servir encore de ce merveilleux plat?	Oso chiederle ancora un po' di questa pietanza squisita?	¿Puedo comer un poco más de este maravilloso plato?
(Pweesh mer sairveer ankor der ser mairvaiyehr plah?)	*(Oh-zoh kee-eh-der-leh ahn-ko-rah oon poh dee kwestah pee-eh-tan-zah skwee-zee-tah?)*	*(Pwéddoh kohmérr oon pókoh máss deh ésteh marah-beellyósoh plátoh?)*
J'espère être digne un jour votre fille.	Spero un giorno di dimos-trarmi degno di sua figlia.	Espero que algún día sea digno de su hija.
(Shaispair aitr deen an shoor der votr feey.)	*(Speh-roh oon johr-noh dee dee-mostrar-mee deh-nee-oh dee soo-ah fee-lee-ah.)*	*(Spéroh ké algoon deeya séah deeknoh deh soo ee-hah.)*
A quelle date pensez-vous partir et pour combien de temps?	Quand'è che vanno via esattamente, e per quanto?	¿Cuándo se marchará usted y por cuánto tiempo?
(A kel dart pansay-voo parteer ay poor combyan der tam?)	*(Kwan-deh keh vahn-noh vee-ah eh-sah-tah-menteh eh per kwantoh tempoh?)*	*(Kwándoh seh marchahrá oostéd ee pór kwántoh tee-yémpoh?)*
J'ai bien peur de ne pouvoir l'épouser, ça ne plairait pas du tout à ma femme.	Temo che proprio non potrei sposarla: mia moglie si opporrebbe.	Siento mucho no poderme casar con ella. Mi mujer se opondría.
(Shay byan pehr der ner poovvahr laipoozay, sahn plairay par di too ar ma famm.)	*(Teh-moh keh proh-pree-oh non poh-treh-ee spoh-sarlah: mee-ah moh-lee-eh see op-por-rehb-beh.)*	*(Seeyéntoh mootchoh noh podérr-meh kahssárr kón ehllya. Mee moohhérr sé opondreeyah.)*

IN THE CAR

These reclining seats are very comfortable.

Diese Liegesitze sind sel bequem.

(Dize ligezitse zind zehr bequaym.

Let me help you with your seat belt.

Komm, ich schnalle Deine Sicherheitsgurt fest.

(Komm, ish shnaalle dynen zishe hytsgoort fest.)

Move your seat back; it's easier.

Es geht leichter, wenn Du Dein Sitz zurückschiebst.

(Es gayt lyshter, venn doo dyn zits tsoorueck-shibst.)

Don't blame my hand; blame the gearshift.

Die Schaltung lässt nicht vi Platz für meine Hände.

(Di shaaltoong laysst nisht plaats fuer myne haynde.)

I'm sorry, my watch got caught in your garter when I put it in third gear.

Entschuldige, beim Schalten i: meine Uhr in Deinem Strump band hängen geblieben.

(Entshooldige, bym shaalten i: myne oor in dynem shtroomfbaan hayngen gebliben.)

FRENCH	ITALIAN	SPANISH
Ces sièges-couchettes sont très confortables.	Questi sedili ribaltabili sono comodissimi.	Éstos asientos abatibles son muy confortables.
(Say syaish-cooshett son ray confortahbl.)	*(Kweh-stee sehdee-lee ree-bahltah-beelee sono como-dee-see-mee.)*	*(Èstoss assyéntoss ahbah-teeb-less són mooy com-fortáb-less.)*
Je vais vous mettre la ceinture de sécurité.	Lasci che le agganci la cintura di sicurezza.	Déjame que te abroche el cinturón de seguridad.
(Sher vay voo metr la santir der saikireetay.)	*(Lah-shee keh leh ah-gahn-chee lah cheen-too-rah dee see-kooretza.)*	*(Déhhah-meh ké teh ah-brótcheh él thintoorón deh segooreedád.)*
Poussez votre siège vers l'arrière, vous serez mieux.	Sposti indietro il sedile, è più facile.	Echa el asiento hacia atrás, es más fácil.
(Poossay votr syaish vair laryair, voo sray myer.)	*(Spost-ee in-dee-ehtro eel seh-dee-leh, eh pew fah-chee-leh.)*	*(Étchah él assyéntoh átheeya ahtráss, ess máss fáthill.)*
Le changement de vitesses ne laisse pas beaucoup de liberté à ma main.	La leva del cambio non mi permette di muovere la mano.	La palanca de cambio no me deja mucho sitio para la mano.
(Ler shanshman der veetaiss ne laiss par bawkood lee-bairtay ar ma man.)	*(Lah leh-vah dehl cahm-bee-o non mee perm-eh-teh dee moo-oh-vehre lah mah-no.)*	*(Lá pahlánkah deh kám-beeyoh noh meh déhhah mootchoh síttyoh párah lá mánoh.)*
Je m'excuse, ma montre s'est accrochée à votre jarretelle pendant que je changeais de vitesse.	Mi dispiace, mi si è impigliato l'orologio nella sua giarrettiera mentre cambiavo marcia.	Lo siento, se me ha enganchado el reloj con tu liga al cambiar de marcha.
(Sher mexkiz, ma montr say takroshay ar votr shartel pandan ker sher shanshayd veetaiss.)	*(Mee dis-pee-a-cheh, mee see eh eem-pee-lee-ah-to l'oroh-lojo neh-la swa jareh-tee-ehrah mehntreh cahm-bee-ahvo march-ah.)*	*(Loh seeyéntoh, seh mé ah engantchádoh él rhelóhh kón too leegah ál kambeeyárr deh márchah.)*

IN THE CAR

There's plenty left when it's on empty.

Es gibt immer noch ziemlich viel wenn der Zeiger auf "leer" steht

(Es gibt immer noch tsimlish fiel venn der tsyger aof "layr" shteht.

I've run out of gas.

Aber jetzt ist der Tank leer.

(Aaber yetst ist der taank layr.)

It looks like the car broke down.

Der Wagen liegt fest.

(Der vaagen ligt fest.)

We're miles from anywhere.

Da ist weit und breit nichts in Aussicht.

(Daa ist vyt oond bryt nishts in aosisht.)

It's my fault you're so cold; the least I can do is get you warm.

Es ist meine Schuld, dass Dich so friert, kann ich Dich wenigstens ein bisschen erwärmen.

(Es ist myne shoold, daas dish zo frirt, kan ish dish venigstens yn bis-shen ervairmen.)

Ne vous inquiétez pas, il y a encore plein d'essence dans le réservoir quand la jauge indique zéro.	Anche quando segna zero c'è ancora una grossa riserva.	Todavía queda mucha, cuando parece que está vacío.
(Ner voo zankyetay par, eelyar ankor plan daissans dan ler raizairvwahr kan la shawsh andeek zairo.)	*(Ahnkeh kwando seh-nya zeh-ro chay ahn-kó-ra oona gross-ah ree-servah.)*	*(Toddabeeyah kéddah mootchah, kwándoh parétheh ké stáh bahtheeyoh.)*
Zut, je n'ai plus d'essence!	Non c'è piú benzina.	Me he quedado sin gasolina.
(Zit, sher nay pli daissans!)	*(Non chay pew benzee-nah.)*	*(Meh eh keddádoh sinn gassoleenah.)*
Il ne manquait plus que ça, on est tombé en panne!	S'è guastata la macchina.	El coche está averiado.
(Eel ner mankay plik sah, onay tombay an pann!)	*(Seh gwah-stata lah makeena.)*	*(El kótcheh stáh abereeyádoh.)*
On est en pleine cambrousse.	Non c'è nulla qui vicino.	Estamos lejos de cualquier sitio.
(Onay tan plenn cambrooce.)	*(Non chay noo-lah kwee vee-chee-no.)*	*(Stámoss léhhoss deh kwalkeeyer síttyoh.)*
Pauvre chou! vous avez froid; comme tout ça est de ma faute, le moins que je puisse faire est de vous tenir chaud.	È colpa mia se hai tanto freddo: il minimo che posso fare è scaldarti.	Es culpa mía que tengas tanto frío; lo menos que puedo hacer es calentarte.
(Pawvr shoo! voo zavay frwar; comm too sah sayd ma fawt, ler mwan kersh pweece fair ay der voo terneer shaw.)	*(Eh colpah mee-ah seh ah-y tahnto freh-do, eel meeneemo keh posso far-reh eh skahl-dartee.)*	*(Ess koolpah meeah ké téngass tántoh freeoh; loh ménoss ké pwéddoh atherr ess kahlentarr-teh.)*

ON THE BUS

I'm so sorry; I thought it was the strap.

Verzeihen Sie, ich dachte es wa die Strippe zum festhalten.

(Fertsyn zi, ish dachte es vaar shtrippe tsoom festhaalten.)

No, I didn't pinch you.

Ich habe die Strippe nicl gekniffen.

(Ish haube dee shtrippe nisht gel kniffen.)

No, I didn't pinch you.

'e m'excuse, je voulais simplement m'attraper à la barre pour ne pas tomber.

(Sher mexkiz, sher voolay amplman matrappay ar la ar poor ner par tombay.)

Scusi, credevo fosse la maniglia.

(Skoo-see, kreh-deh-vo fohse lah mah-nee-lee-ah.)

Lo siento, creí que era un agarradero.

(Loh seeyéntoh, kreeh-ee ké érah oon ahgahrrahdéroh.)

'as du tout, ce n'est pas noi!

Par di too, snay par mwar!)

No, non le ho dato un pizzicotto.

(Noh, non leh oh dah-to oon pee-tzee-cohto.)

No, yo no he sido.

(Noh, yoh noh eh seedoh.)

75

ON THE BUS

In my country, rubbing knees is a sign of courtesy.

Wo ich herkomme, da ist da Kniereiben ein Ausdruck de Höflichkeit.

(Vo ish herkomme, daa ist da kkniryben yn aosdrook der hoeflish kyt.)

IN THE COUNTRY

Let's pick bluebells/roses/daisies/weeds.

Komm, wir pflücken Glocken blumen / Rosen / Gänseblümchen Unkraut.

(Komm, vir pfluecken glocken bloomen / rozen / gaynzeblumshen oonkraot.)

I'm an undercover customs man, and I have to search you for contraband.

Ich bin Zollbeamter in Zivil ich glaube, Sie haben Schmug gelware an sich.

(Ish bin tsollbe-aamter in tsivil ish glaobe, zi haaben shmoogelvaar aan zish.)

Let's sit down on this haystack.

Setzen wir uns doch in de Heuschober.

(Zetsen vir oons doch in de hoyshober.)

Dans mon pays, la politesse eux qu'on se touche les genoux.

Dan mon paiee, la poleetess er konce toosh lay shernoo.)

Al mio paese, toccare il ginocchio è un segno di elementare cortesia.

(Ahl mee-o pah-ehseh toh-kah-reh eel jee-nock-eeo eh oon seh-neeo dee element-ahreh cohr-teh-seeah.)

En mi país frotarse las rodillas es una mera señal de cortesía.

(Én mee pah-is frohtárr-seh lass rhodeellyass ess oonah mérah senyáll de cohrteh-síah.)

Allons cueillir des jacinthes — roses — marguerites — herbes folles.

(Allon keryeer day shasant — rawz — marguereet — airb fol.)

Cogliamo le violette/le rose/ le margherite/ le erbacce.

(Co-lee-amo leh vee-ohleh-teh/leh roseh/leh mar-gueh-ree-teh/leh ehrbah-cheh?)

Cojamos campanillas, rosas, margaritas y hierbecillas.

(Kohhámoss kampahn-eellyass/róssass/margareetass ee yerbehthillyass.)

---

e suis douanier en civil et e veux vérifier si vous n'avez pas sur vous de la contrebande.

(Sher swee dooanyay an eeveel ay sher ver vaireefyay ee voo navay par sir voo der a kontrband.)

Sono un doganiere in borghese e ho motivo di ritenere che nasconda addosso materiale di contrabbando.

(Sonoh oon doh-gah-nee-eh-reh in bor-ghe-seh eh oh motiv-oh dee ree-tehneh-reh keh nah-skon-dah ah-dohso mah-teh-ree-ahleh dee cohn-trah-bahndo.)

Soy un vista de Aduanas de paisano, y creo que lleva contrabando encima.

(Sóy oon beestah de Ad-wánass deh paysánnoh y kréoh ke llyévah contra-bándoh entheemah.)

Oh la belle meule de foin! Allons nous y asseoir un peu.

(Oh la bell merl der fwan! Allon noo zee asswahr an per.)

Sediamoci su questo fienile.

(Seh - dee - ahmochee soo kwestoh fee-ehnee-leh.)

Sentémonos en este pajar.

(Sentémonoss en ésteh pah-hárr.)

IN THE COUNTRY

Let's get away from this crowd and into that tall grass.

Gehen wir doch da drüben in das schöne, hohe Gras, weit weg von den vielen Menschen.

(Gayn vir doch daa drueben in das shoene, hohe graass, vyt vayg fon den filen menshen.)

A bug went down your blouse. I'll get it out.

Ein Käfer ist gerade in Deine Bluse gekrabbelt, aber ich werde ihn schon finden.

(Yn kayfer ist geraade in dyne bloose gecrabbelt, aber ish verde ihn shon finden.)

Lying down is the only way to appreciate the sky.

Im Liegen kann man erst den Himmel richtig geniessen.

(Im liegen kann maan erst den himmel rishtig geniessen.)

There's nobody around, and it's the only real way to swim.

Hier ist doch kein Mensch, so schwimmt man besser.

(Hir ist doch kyn mensh, zo shvimt maan besser.)

Si on quittait toute cette foule pour aller marcher dans cette belle prairie?

(See on keetay toot set fool poor allay marshay dan set bell prairee?)

Allontaniamoci da tutta questa gente; andiamo a passeggiare tra quella bella erba alta.

(Ah-lontah-nee-ah-mochee dah too-tah kwestah jenteh; ahn-dee-ahmo ah pass-eh-jah-reh tra kwelah bellah eh-rbah ah-ltah.)

Huyamos de la multitud y vámonos a aquel prado de hierba alta.

(Ooyámoss de la moolteetood ee bámonoss ah ahkéll prádoh deh yérbah áltah.)

Oh là! il y a une petite bête qui est entrée sous votre chemisier; attendez, je vais la sortir.

(Oh lar! eelyar in pteet bet kee ay tantray soo votr shmeezyay; attanday, sher vay la sorteer.)

Ho visto un insetto correre dentro alla sua camicetta— l'aiuto a cercarlo.

(Oh vee-sto oon inset-toh coh-reh-reh dehntro ah-lah swah cah-mee-cheh-tah — l'ah-yew-toh ah cher-car-loh.)

Se te ha metido un insecto bajo la blusa, déjame que te lo saque.

(Seh teh ah meteedoh oon eenséktoh báhhoh lah bloossah, déhhahmeh ké teh loh sákeh.)

Rien ne vaut de s'étendre sur le dos pour apprécier toute la beauté du ciel!

(Ryan ner vaw der setandr sir le do poor appressyay toot la bawtay di syell!)

È solo sdraiati che si può vedere bene il cielo.

(Eh solo sdrah-yah-tee keh see pwoh veh-deh-reh beneh eel chay-lo.)

La única forma de contemplar el cielo es acostándose.

(Lah ooneekah formah deh kohntemplárr él thiyéloh ess akosstándoseh.)

Il n'y a personne dans les parages et c'est la meilleure façon d'aller dans l'eau.

(Eelnyar pairsonn dan lay parahsh ay say la meyehr farson dallay dan law.)

Siamo proprio soli ed è il miglior modo per nuotare.

(See-ahmo pro-pree-oh solee ehd-ay eel mee-leeor modo per noo-oh-tar-eh.)

No hay nadie por aquí, y esta es la única forma verdadera de nadar.

(Noh áy náddyeh pór akee, ee éstah ess lah ooneekah fórmah berdahdérah deh naddarr.)

IN THE COUNTRY

You look cold; let me warm you up.

Du siehst verfroren aus—komm ich wärme Dich.

(Doo ziest ferfroren aos, komm ish vairme dish.)

Where I come from we're modern about these things.

Da wo ich herkomme, denkt man über diese Dinge sehr modern.

(Da vo ish herkomme, denkt maan ueber diese dinge zehr modairn.)

I brought a tarp just in case the grass is wet.

Ich habe eine Decke, falls das Gras nass ist.

(Ish haabe yne decke, falls das graass nass ist.)

AT THE PARTY

We're out of food, but there's plenty to drink.

Zu Essen gibt's nicht mehr—aber trinken Sie doch.

(Tsoo ayssen gibt's nisht mayr—aber trinken zi doch.)

Are you over sixteen?

Sie sind doch schon sechzehn?

(Zi zind doch shon zaysh-tsehn?)

On dirait que vous avez froid; je vais vous réchauffer un peu.	Si vede che hai freddo. Ti scaldo io.	Creo que tienes frío. Déjame que te caliente.
(On deerayk voo zavay frwar; sher vay voo raishawfay an per.)	*(See veh-deh keh ah-y frehdo. Tee scah-ldoh ee-oh.)*	*(Kréoh ké teeyénness freeyoh. Déhhah-meh ké teh kaleeyénteh.)*

Dans mon pays, on n'est pas vieux jeu; on a des idées modernes à ce sujet.	Al mio paese in queste cose siamo molto moderni.	De donde yo vengo, somos modernos en estas cosas.
(Dan mon paiee, onay par vyer sher; on ar day zeeday modairn ass sishay.)	*(Ahl mee-oh pah-ehseh in kweh-steh coseh see-ahmo molto modern-ee.)*	*(Deh dóndeh yoh béngoh, sómoss modérnoss én éstass kóssas.)*

J'ai un tapis de sol, au cas où l'herbe est mouillée.	L'erba è bagnata, ho portato apposta un impermeabile.	Tengo una esterilla por si la hierba está húmeda.
(Shay an tapee der sol, aw car oo lairb ay mooyay.)	*(L'ehrbah eh ba-nee-ahtah, oh port-ahto ah-postah oon impehr-meh-ahbee-leh.)*	*(Téngoh oonah stehreellyah pór see lah yérbah stáh oomehdah.)*

Il n'y a plus rien à manger, mais prenez un bon verre à la place.	Da mangiare non è rimasto nulla, ma bevi questo invece.	No ha quedado comida, pero en cambio hay mucho para beber.
(Eelnyar pli ryenar manshay, may prernay an bon vair ar la plahs.)	*(Dah mahn-jah-reh non eh ree-mah-sto noo-lah, mah beh-vee kwehsto in-vehcheh.)*	*(Noh ah kehdádoh komeedah, péroh en kámbeeyoh áy mootchoh párah behberr.)*

Je parie que vous n'avez même pas seize ans!?	Ha già compiuto 16 anni?	¿Ha cumplido los dieciséis años?
(Shparee ker voo navay maim par saix an!?)	*(Ah jah com-pew-to seh-dee-chee ah-nee?)*	*(Ah koompleedoh lóss dyéthisséis ányoss?)*

AT THE PARTY

My uncle, Mr. Rockefeller, always says_____.

Mein Onkel Rockefeller sagt immer____

(Myn onkel Rockefeller saagt immer ____)

Let me take you home—to *my* home!

Darf ich Sie zu mir nach Haus begleiten?

(Darf ish zi stoo mir nach haos beglyten?)

It's quieter upstairs in the bedroom.

Oben im Schlafzimmer ist es viel ruhiger.

(Oben im shlaaftsimmer ist es fiel roohiger.)

You have an incredible figure; is it really all you?

Sie haben ja eine tolle Figur; fast schon unnatürlich.

(Zi haaben yaa yne tolle figoor; fast shon oonaatuerlish.)

Prove it.

Beweisen!

(Bevysen!)

I know some great games for adults.

Ich kenne ein paar Spiele für Erwachsene.

(Ish kenne yn paar shpiele fuer ervaaxene.)

FRENCH	ITALIAN	SPANISH
Mon oncle, Monsieur Rockefeller, disait toujours—	Mio zio, il signor Rockefeller, dice sempre che___	Mi tío, Mr. Rockefeller, siempre dice ___
(Mon onkl, Mersyer Rockfellair, deezay tooshoor__)	*(Mee-o tzee-o eel see-nyor Rockefeller, dee-cheh sehmpreh keh ._.—)*	*(Mee tee-oh, Mr. Rockefeller, seeyémpreh deetheh ___)*
Je vais vous ramener chez... moi.	Permetta che l'accompagni a casa—a casa mia.	¿Quiere que la lleve a casa . . . a mi casa?
(Sher vay voo ramnay shay... mwar.)	*(Per-meh-ta keh l'ah-kompah-nee ah cah-sah—ah cah-sah mee-ah.)*	*(Keeyéreh. ké lah llyébeh ah kássah . . . ah mee kássah?)*
C'est plus calme en haut, dans la chambre à coucher.	È piú tranquillo in camera.	Arriba, en el dormitorio, se está más tranquilo.
(Say pli cahlm an aw, dan la shambr ar cooshay.)	*(Eh pew trahn-kwee-lo in camera.)*	*(Ah-ríbbah, én él dormeettórioh, sé stáh máss trahnkeeloh.)*
Vous avez un de ces corps, c'est incroyable! Je parie que c'est du chiqué!	Ha un personale stupendo. Non mi dirà che è tutto naturale?	Tiene usted una silueta estupenda. A lo mejor no es natural.
(Voo zavay an der say kor, setancrwayabl! Sher paree ker say di shickay.)	*(Ah oon person-ah-leh stoopen-do. Non mee dee-rah keh eh too-to nah-too rahleh.)*	*(Teeyénneh oosté oonah siluet-tah stoopéndah. Ah loh mehhórr. noh ess nattooral.)*
Chiche!	Me lo dimostri.	¡Demuéstrelo!
(Sheesh!)	*(Me lo dee-most-ree.)*	*(Dehmwéstreh-loh!)*
Je connais quelques passe-temps pour adultes...	Conosco dei giuochi da adulti.	Sé algunos juegos para mayores.
(Shkonnay kelk passtan poor adilt...)	*(Co-no-sco day jew-okee dah ah-dooltee.)*	*(Sé ahlgoonoss hooéghoss párah mah-yóress.)*

AT THE DANCE

May I have the pleasure of this dance?

Darf ich um diesen Tanz bitten?
(Darf ish oom disen taans bitten?)

Oh, you'll do.

O—Sie sind o.k!
(o, zi zind o.k!)

Great band, isn't it?

Die Kapelle ist gut, nicht wahr?
(Di kapelle ist good, nisht vaar?)

Do you come here often?

Sind Sie oft hier?
(Zind si oft hir?)

I'm sorry my hand slipped.

Verzeihung, meine Hand ist gerutscht.
(Fertsy-oong, myne haand ist gerootsht.)

May I take you home?

Darf ich Sie nach Hause begleiten?
(Daarf ish zi naach haose beglyten?)

Let's go, kid.

Gehen wir, Kleine.
(Gehen vir, klyne.)

FRENCH	ITALIAN	SPANISH
M'accorderez-vous cette danse? *(Macordray-voo set dans?)*	Posso avere il piacere di questo ballo? *(Possoh ah-veh-reh eel pee-ah-cheh-reh dee kwestoh bahl-loh?)*	¿Me permites este baile? *(Meh permítess ésteh báyleh?)*
Mmm... ça ira. *(Mmm... sar eerah.)*	Su, andiamo? *(Soo, ahn-dee-ah-moh?)*	¡Oh! Tú me vas. *(Oh! Too meh báss.)*
Il est bien l'orchestre, n'est-ce pas? *(Eel ay byan lorchestr, naispar?)*	Bell'orchestrina, no? *(Behl - lor - keh - streenah, noh?)*	Buena orquesta, ¿verdad? *(Bwénah orkessta, berdath?)*
Vous venez souvent ici? *(Voo vnay soovan eecee?)*	Lei viene qui spesso? *(Leh-ee vee-eh-neh kwee speh-soh?)*	¿Vienes a menudo por aquí? *(Beeyénness ah mehnoodoh pór akee?)*
Oh, pardon! ma main a glissé...! *(Oh, pardon! ma man ar gleessay...!)*	Scusi, mi è scivolata la mano. *(Skoo-zee, mee eh shee-voh-lah-tah lah mah-noh.)*	Lo siento. Me ha resbalado la mano. *(Loh seeyéntoh. Meh ah ressbahládoh lah mánoh.)*
Puis-je vous raccompagner chez vous? *(Pweesh voo racompanyay shay voo?)*	Posso accompagnarla a casa? *(Possoh ak-kom-pah-nee-ar-lah ah kah-sah?)*	¿Puedo Acompañarte a casa? *(Pwéddoh akompanyarrteh ah kássah?)*
Allez, viens, Poupée! *(Allay, vyan, Poopay!)*	Andiamo via, bambola. *(Ahn-dee-ah-moh vee-ah, bahm-bolah.)*	¡Vámonos, niña! *(Bámonoss, neenyah!)*

AT THE DANCE

I'm not a good dancer, but I like holding women.

Ich bin zwar kein guter Tänzer, aber ich halte gerne Frauen im Arm.

(Ish bin tsvar kyn gooter tayntser, aber ish haalte gairne fraon im arm.)

Dancing closer is in style these days.

Eng tanzen ist viel schicker.

(Eng tantsen ist fil shicker.)

It's too warm; let's get some fresh air.

Es ist sehr warm hier; schnappen wir doch ein bisschen frische Luft draussen.

(Es ist zehr varm hir; schnaappen vir doch yn bis-shen frishe looft draossen.)

Let me get you something to drink.

Soll ich Ihnen einen Fruchtsaft oder so 'was ähnliches holen?

(Zol ish ihnen ynen froochtzaft oder zo 'vas aynlishes holen?)

Take your girdle off and have some fun.

Zieh' Deinen Hüftgürtel aus und amüsiere Dich.

(Tsih dynen hueftguertel aos oond amuezire dish.)

FRENCH	ITALIAN	SPANISH
Je ne suis pas un as de la piste, mais, j'aime bien tenir une femme dans mes bras. *(Shern swee pazanass der la peest, may shaym byan terneer in famm dan may brah.)*	Non ballo bene, ma mi piace avere una donna tra la braccia. *(Non bahl-loh beh-neh, mah mee pee-ah-cheh ah-veh-reh oo-nah don-nah trah leh brah-cha.)*	No bailo muy bien, pero me gusta abrazar a las mujeres. *(Noh báyloh mooy beeyén, péroh mé goostah abrathár ah lass moohhéress.)*
Danser corps à corps, ça a tellement plus de style. *(Dansay korakor, sar ar tellman pli der steel.)*	E tanto piú elegante ballare stretti stretti. *(Èh tahn-toh pew eleganteh bahl - lah - reh streht - tee streht-tee.)*	Bailar muy juntos es más elegante. *(Baylár mooy hoontoss ess máss ellegánteh.)*
Il fait trop chaud, sortons un peu prendre l'air. *(Eel fay tro shaw, sorton an per prandr lair.)*	Fa troppo caldo, andiamo a prendere una boccata d'aria. *(Fah trop-poh kahl-doh, ahn-dee-ah-moh ah prendeh-reh oo-nah bok-kah-tah dah-reeah.)*	Hace mucho calor; salgamos a tomar el fresco. *(Atheh mootchoh kahlór; salgámoss ah tohmár él frésskoh.)*
Voulez-vous un jus de fruit ou une boisson quelconque…? *(Voolay-voo an shi der frwee oo in bwahson kelkonk…?)*	Permetta che le offra una spremuta o qualche altra cosa? *(Permeht-tah keh leh offrah oo-nah spreh-moo-tah oh kwal-keh ahl-trah kohsah.)*	¿Quieres un zumo de frutas o algo? *(Keeyéress oon thoomoh dé frootass oh álgoh?)*
Enlève donc ta gaîne et mets-toi à l'aise! *(Anlaiv donk ta gain ay may-twar ar laiz!)*	Si metta in libertà e si diverta. *(See met-tah een lee-bertàh eh see dee-vehr-tah.)*	Quítate el cinturón y te sentirás mejor. *(Keetáteh él thintoorón ee teh senteeráss mehhór.)*

AT THE DANCE

In this dance, that's where my hand has to be.

Bei diesem Tanz muss die eine Hand da sein.

(By disem tants moos di yne haand daa syn.)

Let me teach you a special dance.

Soll ich Dir einen ganz tollen Tanz beibringen?

(Zol ish dir ynen gaans tollen tants bybringen?)

GAMBLING

My name is _____, and I just won you.

Meine Name ist _____ ich habe Sie gerade gewonnen.

(Myn naame ist _____ Ish haabe zi geraade gevonnen.)

Let's play strip poker.

Spielen wir Strip-Poker.

(Shpielen vir strip-poker.)

Let's play strip blackjack.

Spielen wir Strip-Vingt-et-un.

(Shpielen vir strip-vingt-ay-ong.)

FRENCH	ITALIAN	SPANISH
Pour cette danse, il faut qu'une main soit placée en cet endroit. *(Poor set dans, eel faw kin man swar playsay an set andrwar.)*	Ma in questo ballo bisogna tenere una mano lí. *(Mah een kewstoh bahl-loh bee-zoh-neeah teh-neh-reh oo-nah mah-noh lée.)*	En este baile, una mano debe ponerse aquí. *(Enn ésteh báyleh, oonah mánoh débeh ponérseh akee.)*
Je vais vous apprendre un genre spécial de danse. *(Sher vay voo zaprandr an shanr spaisyal der dans.)*	Lasci che le insegni un ballo speciale. *(Lah-shee keh leh een-seh-nee oon bahl-loh speh-chee-ah-leh.)*	¿Quieres que te enseñe un nuevo baile? *(Keeyéress ké té ensényeh oon nwéboh báyleh?)*
Je m'appelle _____ Je viens de vous gagner au jeu. *(Sher mappell _____ Sher vyan der voo ganyay aw sher.)*	Mi chiamo _____ e ho vinto lei come premio. *(Mee kee-ah-mo _____ eh o veen-to lay comeh preh-mee-o.)*	Me llamo _____ y acabo de ganarla a usted. *(Meh llyámoh _____ ee ahkáboh deh gahnárr-lah ah oostéh.)*
Si on faisait un strip-poker? *(See on ferzay an streep-pokair?)*	Giuochiamo a poker con lo spogliarello. *(Jew-oh-kee-ah-mo ah poker kon lo spo-lee-ah-rehlo.)*	Juguemos al poker con nuestra ropa. *(Hoogémoss ál poker kón nwéstrah rópah.)*
Si on faisait une partie de strip-vingt-et-un? *(See on ferzay in partee der streep-vantai-an?)*	Giuochiamo a sette e mezzo con lo spogliarello. *(Jew-oh-kee-ah-mo ah sehteh eh meh-tzo kon lo spo-lee-ah-rehlo.)*	Juguemos al pontoon con nuestra ropa. *(Hoogémoss á! pontoon kón nwéstrah rópah.)*

GAMBLING

Let's play strip bridge.

Spielen wir Strip-Bridge.

(Shpielen vir strip-bridge.)

No, you can't have your clothes back.

Nein, die Sachen kriegen Sie nicht wieder.

(Nyn, di zaachen kriegen zi nisht vieder.)

Let's play strip bridge.

FRENCH	ITALIAN	SPANISH
On va faire une partie de strip-bridge!	Giuochiamo a bridge: chi perde si spoglia.	Juguemos al bridge con nuestra ropa.
(On var fair in partee der streep-breedge!)	*(Jew - oh - kee - ah - mo ah bridge. Kee pehr-deh see spo-leeah.)*	*(Hoogémoss ál bridge kón nwéstrah rópah.)*
Je suis désolé, les vêtements enlevés ne se reprennent plus!	No, non te li restituisco.	No, eso me lo quedo en prenda.
(Sher swee daizolay, lay vetman anlvay ner ser rerpren pli!)	*(No, non teh lee reh-stee-too-eesko.)*	*(Noh, éssoh meh loh kédoh en préndah.)*

IN THE BAR

Is this seat taken?

Ist dieser Platz besetzt?
(Ist diser plaats bezetst?)

Two large gins, please.

Zwei doppelte Gin, bitte.
(Tsvy doppelte Gin, bitte.)

It's only a small drink—almost all fruit juice.

Das soll ein doppelter sein? Ist ja fast alles Fruchtsaft.
(Daas zoll yn doppelter zyn? ist yaa faast alles froochtsaaft.)

You drink too slowly!

Du trinkst ja sehr langsam.
(Doo trinkst yaa zehr laangzaam.)

We can both squeeze in over there.

Wir können uns da noch gerade zwischensetzen.
(Vir koennen oons daa nock geraade tsvishen zetsen.)

Hold onto me.

Kannst Dich an mich lehnen.
(Kannst dish aan mish laynen.)

FRENCH	ITALIAN	SPANISH
Il y a quelqu'un à cette place? *(Eelyah kelkan ar set plahs?)*	È libero questo posto? *(Eh lee-beh-roh kwestoh poh-stoh?)*	¿Está ocupado este asiento? *(Stáh okoopádoh ésteh assyéntoh?)*
Deux grands gins, s'il vous plaît! *(Dehr gran gin, seel voo play.)*	Due doppi gin per favore. *(Doo-eh dop-pee gin per fah-voh-reh.)*	Dos ginébras dobles, por favor. *(Dóss heenébrass dób-less, pór fahbór.)*
Allez, c'est tout petit et il n'y a pratiquement que du jus de fruit. *(Allay, say too pertee ay eel nyah prateekman ker di shi der frwee.)*	Ma no, è quasi tutto succo di frutta. *(Mah noh, eh kwazee toottoh sook-koh dee froot-tah.)*	Hay muy poquito, casi todo es zumo de frutas. *(Ay mooy pokeetoh, kássy tóddoh ess thoomoh dé frootass.)*
Vous buvez à peine et si lentement! *(Voo bivay ar pain ay see lantman.)*	Sta bevendo molto lentamente. *(Stah beh-vendoh moltoh len-tah-menteh.)*	Bebes muy despacio. *(Bébess mooy despáthioh.)*
Il y a là-bas une place pour nous deux, en nous serrant un peu. *(Eelyah lah-bah in plahs poor noo dehr, an noo serran an pehr.)*	Ci stiamo tutti e due in quell'angolino là. *(Chee stee-ah-moh toot-tee eh doo-eh een kwell an-goh-lee-noh lah.)*	Todavía cabemos los dos, estrechándonos un poco. *(Toddabíah kahbémoss lóss dóss, stretchándonoss oon pókoh.)*
Je vais vous soutenir. *(Sher vay voo sootneer.)*	Si appoggi a me. *(See ap-poh-jee ah meh.)*	Déjame que te aguante. *(Déhhah-meh ké teh agwánteh.)*

IN THE BAR

I like beer best; it's cheaper too.

Am liebsten trinke ich Bier; ist auch billiger.

(*Am libsten trinke ish beer; ist aoch billiger.*)

Try a rum in your beer, dear.

Probiere doch 'mal einen Rum im Bier, Kleine.

(*Probire doch 'maal ynen roomm im beer, klyne.*)

Of course I'm not trying to get you drunk.

Ich will Dir doch keinen Schwips andrehen!

(*Ish vill dir doch kynen shvips andrehen!*)

Why don't you try something different?

Trinke 'mal etwas anderes.

(*Trinke 'maak etvaas aanderes.*)

I'd better see you home safely.

Ist wohl besser, wenn ich Dich nach Hause bringe.

(*Ist vol besser, venn ish dish nach haoze bringe.*)

FRENCH	ITALIAN	SPANISH

e trouve que la bière, c'est
e qu'il y a de meilleur—et
uis c'est bien moins cher!

*Sher troov ker la byair, say
keelyah der maiyehr—ay
wee say byan mwan shair.)*

Io preferisco sempre la
birra—e costa anche meno.

*(Ee - oh preh - feh - reeskoh
sehm-preh lah beer-rah—
eh koh-stah ahn-keh meh-
noh.)*

Siempre me ha parecido
mejor la cerveza . . . y más
barata también.

*(Seeyémpreh meh ah pare-
theedoh mehhór lah zer-
béthah . . . ee máss bahrátah
tambeeyén.)*

Essayez donc un petit verre
le rhum dans votre bière.

*Essayay donk an ptee vair
ler rom dan votr byair.)*

Aggiungiamo un po' di
rum alla birra, cara.

*(Ah-jewn-jah-moh oon poh
dee room ahl-lah beer-rah,
cah-rah.)*

Ponte un poquito de ron en
la cerveza, querida.

*(Pónteh oon pokeetoh deh
rhón én lá zerbéthah,
kehreedah.)*

3ien sûr que non, je ne
cherche pas du tout à vous
aoûler!

*Byan sir ker non, shern
hairsh par di too ar voo
oolay!)*

Non è vero che sto cer-
cando di ubriacarti.

*(Non eh veh-roh keh stoh
chair-can-doh dee oo-bree-
ah-kartee.)*

Por supuesto, no trato de
emborracharte.

*(Pórr sooppwéstoh, noh
tráttoh deh embohrrahchár-
teh.)*

Prenez autre chose, main-
tenant.

*Prernay awtr shawz,
mantnan.)*

Ora prendi qualcosa di
diverso.

*(Orah prehn-dee kwal-koh-
zah dee dee-ver-soh.)*

Ahora probemos algo
diferente.

*(Ah-órah prohbémoss álgoh
differénteh.)*

Il vaut mieux que je vous
accompagne jusque chez
vous.

*Eel vaw myehr ker sher voo
acompahn shisk shay voo.)*

Sarà meglio che l'accom-
pagni a casa.

*(Sarah meh-lee-oh keh lah-
kom-pah-nee ah kah-sah.)*

Será mejor que te lleve a
casa.

*(Seráh mehhórr ké té llyébeh
ah kásah.)*

PRESENTS FOR HER

Where is the ladies' lingerie depart-ment?

Wo ist die Abteilung für Damen unterwäsche?

(Vo ist di abtyloong fuer daamen oonterwayshe?)

Haven't you anything more interesting?

Haben Sie nichts interessanteres

(Haaben zi nishts interessaan teres?)

Bikini.

Bikini.

(Bikini.)

See-through nightie.

Durchsichtiges Nachthemd.

(Doorsh-zishtiges naachthemd.)

See-through slip.

Hauchdünner Unterrock.

(Haochduenner oonterock.)

G-string.

Eine Art Feigenblatt.

(Yne art fygenblatt.)

Tassels.

Quasten.

(Quaasten.)

FRENCH	ITALIAN	SPANISH
Où est le rayon des sous-êtements féminins?	Dov'è il reparto biancheria femminile?	¿Dónde está el departamento de señoras?
Oo ayl rayon day soo-etman faimeenan?)	*(Dovéh eel reh-part-oh bee-ahn-key-ryah feh-mee-nee-leh?)*	*(Dóndeh stáh el departahméntoh deh sehnyórass?)*
Vous n'avez pas quelque hose de plus intéressant?	Non ha proprio nulla di piú interessante?	¿No tiene algo más interesante?
Voo navay par kelk shawz er pli zanterressan?)	*(Non ah propree-o noo-lah dee pew inter-eh-sahn-teh?)*	*(Noh teeyénne álgoh máss interehssánteh?)*
Un bikini.	Bikini.	Bikini.
An beekeenee.)	*(Bikini.)*	*(Beekeenee.)*
Une chemise de nuit transparente.	Una camicia da notte trasparente.	Camisones vaporosos.
In shmeez der nwee trans-ahrant.)	*(Oona cah-mee-chah dah no-teh trah-spah-rehnteh.)*	*(Kahmeessón-ness bapoh-rósoss.)*
Une combinaison transparente.	Una sottoveste trasparente.	Bragas transparentes.
In combeenaizon trans-ehrant.)	*(Oona sotto-vest-eh trah-spah-rehnteh.)*	*(Brágass transpahréntess.)*
Un cache-sexe.	Minimum.	Taparrabos de vedette.
An cash-sex.)	*(Minim-oom.)*	*(Tahpah-rráboss deh veh-détteh.)*
Des franfreluches.	Nappine.	Borlas.
Day franfrerlish.)	*(Nah-pee-neh.)*	*(Bórlass.)*

PRESENTS FOR HER

Baby-doll pajamas.

Babydoll-Pyjamas.
(Babydoll-pyjamas.)

Costume jewelry.

Künstlicher Schmuck.
(Kuenstlisher shmoock.)

Imitation diamonds.

Imitierte Diamanten.
(Imitirte diaamaanten.)

Fancy garters.

Verzierte Strumpfbänder.
(Fertsirte shtroomfbender.)

See-through panties.

Hauchdünne Höschen.
(Haochduenne hoes-shen.)

Push-up bra.

Tiefausgeschnittener B.H.
(Tief-aosgeshnittener bay haa.)

n babydoll.	Babydolls.	Pijamas de muñequita.
4n babeedol.)	*(Babydolls.)*	*(Peehhámmass deh moon-yekeetah.)*
u toc.	Bigiotteria.	Bisutería (joyería).
)i tock.)	*(Bee-jot-err-yah.)*	*(Beessootery-ah (hoy-yery-ah).)*
)u strass.	Diamanti falsi.	Diamantes de imitación.
Di strass.)	*(Dee-ah-mahntee fahl-see.)*	*(Deeahmántess deh imitah-thión.)*
es jarretelles fantaisie.	Giarrettiere fantasia.	Ligas de fantasía.
Day shartell fantaizee.)	*(Jar-reh-tee-ehreh fahn-tah-see-ah.)*	*(Lee-gass deh phantasy-ah.)*
n slip transparent.	Mutandine trasparenti.	Pantaloncitos calados.
4n sleep transpahran.)	*(Moo-tahn-deeneh trah-spah-rehntee.)*	*(Pantahlonthitoss kaládoss.)*
n balconet.	Reggiseno scollato.	Medios sostenes sin tirantes.
4n balkonay.)	*(Reh-jee-sehno skol-lah-to.)*	*(Mehddyoss sosténess seen teerántess.)*

PRESENTS FOR HER

Perfumes.	Parfüm. *(Paarfuem.)*
Bath oil.	Bade-Essenz. *(Baade-essence.)*

SOME USEFUL EXPRESSIONS

My wife doesn't understand me.	Meine Frau versteht mich nich *(Myne frao fershteht mish nisht.*
Let me help you zip that up.	Komm, ich mache Dir d Zipp zu. *(Komm, ish maache dir dayn zi tsoo.)*
It's all right; I'll sleep on the sofa.	Das geht; ich schlafe auf de Sofa. *(Das gayt; ish shlaafe aof de sofa.)*
Let's just cuddle.	Nur 'mal drücken. *(Noor 'maal druecken.)*

FRENCH	ITALIAN	SPANISH
u parfum. *)i parfam.)*	Profumi. *(Pro-foo-mee.)*	Perfumes. *(Perfoomess.)*
ssence de bain. *:ssans der ban.)*	Essenze da bagno. *(Essen-tzeh dah bah-nyo.)*	Colonia para el baño. *(Kolóneeyah párah el bányoh.)*
Ia femme ne me comprend is. *Ma famm ner mer kompran ir.)*	Mia moglie non mi capisce. *(Mee-ah mo-lee-eh non mee cah-pee-sheh.)*	Mi mujer no me comprende. *(Mee moohhérr noh meh kompréndeh.)*
aisse-moi te tirer ta rmeture-éclair. *Laiss-mwar ter teeray ta iirmtir-ecklair.)*	Lasci che l'aiuti a chiudere la cerniera lampo. *(Lah-shee keh l'ah-yew-tee ah kew-deh-reh lah chair-nee-ehrah lahm-po.)*	Déjame que te abroche la cremallera. *(Déhhah-meh ké teh ahbrót-cheh lah crehmahllyérah.)*
'accord, je dormirai sur divan. *Dackor, sher dormeeray sir r deevan.)*	Non si preoccupi: io dormo sul divano. *(Non see preh-ohccoo-pee, yo dormoh sool dee-vahno.)*	Está bien. Dormiré en el diván. *(Stáh beeyén. Dormeeréh én él deebán.)*
implement te prendre ans mes bras! *Smplman ter prandr dan ay brah!)*	Solo un abbraccio. *(Solo oon ah-brah-choh.)*	Un abrazo solamente. *(Oon ahbráthoh solahménteh.)*

SOME USEFUL EXPRESSIONS

Honestly, I tried to reserve single rooms.

Wirklich, ich habe versucht, Ei zelzimmer zu bekommen.

(Virklish, ish haabe ferzooch yntsel-tsimmer tsoo bekommen.)

This is a dangerous town, but I'll protect you.

Das ist eine ganz gefährlicl Stadt, aber ich werde Di beschützen.

(Das ist yne gaants gefairlisl shtadt, aber ish verde dish b shuetsen.)

Let's do it another way.

Versuchen wir es doch einmal s

(Ferzoochen vir es doch ynma zo.)

Your seams aren't straight.

Deine Nähte sind nicht gerade.

(Dyne nayte zind nisht geraade.)

I got carried away.

Ich konnte mich nicht ga beherrschen.

(Ish konnte mish nisht gaa behairshen.)

Where is your birthmark?

Wo ist Dein Muttermal?

(Vo ist dyn mootter-maal?)

FRENCH	ITALIAN	SPANISH

e te jure, j'ai essayé de éserver des chambres à un it!

Shter shir, shay essayay der aizairvay day shambr ar an ee!)

Davvero, ho cercato di prenotare due camere separate.

(Dah-vehro, oh chair-kahto dee preh-notah-reh doo-eh camereh sepa-rahteh.)

¡Palabra! Quería alquilar habitaciones individuales.

(Pahlábrah! Kehreeya ahlkeelárr ahbeetathióness eendeebeeduál-less.)

C'est une ville de gangsters, mais je te protègerai.

(Saitan veel der gangstair, nay shter protaishray.)

Questa è una città pericolosa, ma ti proteggo io.

(Kwehsta eh oona chee-tàh per-ee-kolosa, mah tee proteh-goh yo.)

Esta ciudad es peligrosa, pero yo te protegeré.

(Estah thewdád ess pehlleegrósah, péroh yoh teh protehheréh.)

Si on faisait ça d'une autre manière?

(See on ferzay sah din awtr manyair?)

Proviamo in un altro modo.

(Pro-vee-ahmo in oon ahltro modo.)

Probemos de otra manera.

(Probbémoss deh ótrah mannérah.)

Tes coutures ne sont pas droites!

(Tay cootir ner son par drwat.)

Hai la cucitura delle calze storta.

(Ah-y lah koo-chee-too-rah deh-leh cahl-tzeh stor-tah.)

Tus costuras no son rectas.

(Toos costoorass noh són rréktass.)

Je n'ai pas pu me contrôler!

(Sher nay par pim controlay!)

Ho perso la testa.

(Oh per-so lah teh-stah.)

He perdido los estribos.

(Eh perdeedoh loss streeboss.)

Montre-moi ton «envie».

(Montr-mwar ton «anvee».)

Dove hai un neo?

(Doveh ah-y oon neh-o?)

¿Dónde tienes otro lunar?

(Dóndeh teeyénnes ótroh loonárr?)

SOME USEFUL EXPRESSIONS

I'm afraid of the dark.

Ich fürchte mich im Dunkeln.

(Ish fuershte mish im doonkeln.)

I'm very rich.

Ich bin sehr reich.

(Ish bin zehr rysh.)

Of course I'll write and send for you.

Natürlich schreibe ich Dir, wann
Du nachkommen sollst.

*(Natuerlish shrybe ish dir, van
doo naachkommen zollst.)*

Never mind; I'll get you a new pair.

Macht ja nichts, ich kaufe Dir
ein neues Paar.

*(Macht yaa nishts, ish kaofe dir yn
noyes paar.)*

Come over here.

Komm hier her.

(Komm hier hair.)

Get undressed.

Zieh' Dich aus.

(Tsih dish aos.)

Smith, spelled S-M-I-T-H.

Schmidt, buchstabiert
S–C–H–M–I–D–T.

*(Shmitt, boochshtabirt
es-tsay-haa-em-i-day-tay.)*

I leave in the morning.

Ich fahre morgen Früh.

(Ish faare morgen frue.)

FRENCH	ITALIAN	SPANISH

'ai peur du noir!

Shay pehr di nwahr.)

Ho paura del buio.

(Oh pah-oorah dehl boo-yo.)

Tengo miedo a la oscuridad.

(Téngoh meeyéddoh ah lah oskooreedád.)

---

e suis très riche!

Sher swee tray reesh!)

Io sono ricchissimo.

(Yo sono ree-kee-ssee-moh.)

Soy muy rico.

(Sóy mooy rickoh.)

$ien sûr que je t'écrirai our te dire de venir.

Byan sir kersh teckreeray oor ter deer der verneer.)

Certo che ti scriverò e ti farò venire.

(Chehr-to keh tee scree-vehròh eh tee fah-róh veh-nee-reh.)

Desde luego, te escribiré y te mandaré llamar.

(Désdeh lwégoh, teh scree-biréh ee teh mahndah-réh llyámárr.)

$a ne fait rien, je 'achèterai une autre.

Sarn fay ryan, sher ashetray in awtr.)

Non preoccupati, te ne compro un altro paio.

(Non pre-oc-coopahrtee, teh neh compro oon ahl-troh pah-yo.)

No importa, te compraré otro par.

(Noh eempórtah, teh com-prah-réh ótroh párr.)

Viens par ici.

Vyan pahr eecee.)

Vieni qui.

(Vee-eh-nee kwee.)

Ven por aquí.

(Béhn pór akee.)

)éshabille-toi!

Daizabeey-twar!)

Spogliati.

(Spoh-lee-ahtee.)

Desnúdate.

(Dessnoodah-teh.)

---

e m'appelle Smith, -M–I–T–H–

Sher mapell Smith, ESS– M–EE–TAY–ASH.)

Smith, che si scrive S–M–I–T–H–.

(Smith, keh see scree-veh S–M–I–T–H.)

Smith, deletreado S–M–I–T–H.

(Smith, dehlehtreh-ádoh S–M–I–T–H.)

---

e pars demain matin.

Sher pahr derman matan.)

Parto domattina.

(Part-oh do-mah-teenah.)

Me marcho por la mañana.

(Meh márchoh pór lá mahnyánah.)

SOME USEFUL EXPRESSIONS

I'm being sent on a secret mission with no forwarding address.

Ich habe einen Geheimauftrag kann keine Adresse geben.

(Ish haabe ynen gehym-aoftraag kan kyne adresse gayben.)

FINDING OUT

Do you?

Willst Du?
(Villst doo?)

Shall we?

Sollen wir?
(Zollen vir?)

How about it?

Wie wär's?
(Vi vair's?)

Let's.

Lass' uns doch.
(Laass oons doch.)

Why not?

Warum nicht?
(Varoom nisht?)

Try it.

Versuch's doch 'mal.
(Fersooch's doch 'maal.)

When?

Wann?
(Vaan?)

Where?

Wo?
(Vo?)

FRENCH	ITALIAN	SPANISH

e suis en mission secrète et e ne peux pas te donner l'adresse.

Sher swee zan meesyon ercrett ay shern per par ter lonnay dadress.)

Vado in missione segreta, senza indirizzo.

(Vah-do in miss-yo-neh seh-gretah sehn-tzah in-dee-ree-tzoh.)

Me mandan a una misión secreta, sin domicilio postal.

(Meh mándann ah oonah misión sehcrétah, seen domeethilioh postál.)

Alors...?

Alor...?)

Vuoi?

(Voo-oh-ee?)

¿Quieres?

(Keeyéress?)

Oui...?

Wee...?)

Vogliamo?

(Voh-lee-ah-moh?)

¿Lo haremos?

(Loh ahrémoss?)

Tu veux bien?

Ti ver byan?)

Che ne diresti?

(Keh neh dee-reh-stee?)

¿Qué te parece?

(Ké teh pahrétheh?)

Allons, voyons...!

Alon, vwahyon...!)

Sí?

(See?)

¿Vamos?

(Bámoss?)

Pourquoi pas?

Poorkwar par?)

Perchè no?

(Per-kèh noh?)

¿Por qué no?

(Pór ké noh?)

Essaie!

Essay!)

Prova.

(Proh-vah.)

¡Prueba!

(Prwébbah!)

Quand?

Kan?)

Quando?

(Kwan-doh?)

¿Cuándo?

(Kwándoh?)

Où ça?

Oo sah?)

Dove?

(Doh-veh?)

¿Dónde?

(Dóndeh?)

Love you? Of course I love you. We're in bed again, aren't we?

Ob ich Dich liebe? Natürlic
Wir sind doch schon wieder i
Bett, nicht wahr?

*(Ob ish dish lihbe? naatuerlis
vir zind doch shon vider im be
nisht vaar?)*

You are so beautiful that I don't trust myself to be alone with you.

Ich kann für nichts garantiere
wenn ich mit Dir allein bin—D
bist viel zu verführerisch.

*(Ish kaan fuer nishts gaarantire
ven ish mit Dir alyn bin—doo b
feel tsso ferfuererish.)*

Love you? Of course I love you. We're in bed again aren't we?

FRENCH

Si je t'aime? Bien sûr que je t'aime! Ne suis-je pas en train de te le prouver encore une fois, dans ce lit?

(Seesh taim? Byan sir kersh taim! Ner sweesh pazan tran der terl proovay ankor in fwar, dan slee?)

Tu es si belle que je ne me fais pas confiance, seul avec toi.

(Ti ay see bell ker shern mer fay par confyans, serl aveck twar.)

ITALIAN

Se ti amo? Certo che ti amo, siamo di nuovo a letto insieme, no?

(Seh tee amoh? Chair-toh keh tee amoh, see-ah-moh dee noo-oh-voh ah let-toh eensee-eh-meh, noh?)

Lei è così bella che quando siamo soli ho paura di fare delle pazzie.

(Leh-ee eh ko-zée bella keh kwandoh see-ah-moh sohlee oh pah-oo-rah dee fareh dehl-leh patzee-eh.)

SPANISH

¿Si te quiero? !Claro que te quiero! ¿No estamos otra vez en la cama?

(See teh keeyéroh? Clároh ké teh keeyéroh! Noh stámos ótrah béth én lá kámah?)

Eres tan bonita que no me fío de estar a solas contigo.

(Eres tán bohneetah ké noh meh feeyoh dé star ah sólas konteegoh.)

PET NAMES

Nice piece (of skirt).

Süsses Luder.
(Zuesses looder.)

Honeybunch.

Affenschwänzchen.
(Aaffen-shvayns-shen.)

Apple of my eye.

Augapfel.
(Aogaap-fel.)

Heartthrob.

Herzenswunsch.
(Hairtsens-voonsh.)

Lovebird.

Betthäschen.
(Betthays-shen.)

Angel.

Engelchen.
(Angel-shen.)

Gorgeous.

Bezaubernde.
(Betsaobernde.)

Raving beauty.

Grosse Schönheit.
(Grosse shoenhyt.)

My darling.

Goldstück.
(Goldshtueck.)

FRENCH	ITALIAN	SPANISH
Petit bout de jupon.	Un bel pezzo di ragazza.	Perita en dulce.
(Pertee bood shipon.)	*(Oon behl peh-tzo dee rah-gahtzah.)*	*(Pehreetah en doolzeh.)*
Mon petit chou à la crème.	Dolce tesoro.	Cachito de miel.
(Mon ptee shoo ar la craim.)	*(Dol-cheh teh-so-ro.)*	*(Katcheetoh deh meeyell.)*
Prunelle de mes yeux.	Pupilla dei miei occhi.	Niñita de mis ojos.
(Prinell der may zyer.)	*(Poo-pee-llah day mee-eh-ee okkee.)*	*(Neenyeetah deh mees óhhoss.)*
Amour de mon cœur.	Cuore mio.	Deseo de mi corazon.
(Amoor der mon ker.)	*(Coo-oh-reh mee-o.)*	*(Dehseh-oh deh mee korahthón.)*
Mon petit poulet.	Pulcino adorato.	Palomita.
(Mon ptee poolay.)	*(Pool-chee-no ah-dorah-to.)*	*(Pahlohmeetah.)*
Mon ange.	Angelo mio.	Angel de amor.
(Mon ansh.)	*(Ahn-jeh-lo mee-o.)*	*(Ahn-ghell deh ahmórr.)*
Madone.	Seducente.	Hermosa mía.
(Mahdonn.)	*(Seh-doo-chen-teh.)*	*(Ermóssah meeyah.)*
Beauté du diable.	Bellezza rara.	Belleza delirante.
(Bawtay di deeabl.)	*(Beh-leh-tzah rah-rah.)*	*(Bellyéthah deliránteh.)*
Mon bijou.	Gioia mia.	Mi bella amada.
(Mon beeshoo.)	*(Joy-ah mee-ah.)*	*(Mee béllyah ahmádah.)*

PET NAMES

True love.

Grosse Liebe.
(Grosse liebe.)

Sweetie pie.

Süsse.
(Zuesse.)

Light of my life.

Meine Sonne.
(Myne zonne.)

Dearest.

Liebling.
(Liebling.)

Precious.

Teures.
(Toyres.)

Cupcake.

Puppe.
(Pooppe.)

Lovey-dovey.

Flamme.
(Flamme.)

Lover girl.

Liebchen.
(Liebshen.)

Foxy lady.

Kesse Biene.
(Kaysse biene.)

FRENCH	ITALIAN	SPANISH
Amour de ma vie. *(Amoor de mar vee.)*	Unico amore. *(Oon-ee-ko ah-mo-reh.)*	Amor mío. *(Ahmórr meeyoh.)*
Mon sucre d'orge. *(Mon sikr dorsh.)*	Stellina. *(Steh-lee-nah.)*	Bombón. *(Bombón.)*
Lumière de ma vie. *(Limyair der mar vee.)*	Sole della mia vita. *(Soleh deh-lah mee-ah vee-tah.)*	Luz de mi vida. *(Looth deh mee beedah.)*
Chérie. *(Shairee.)*	Carissima. *(Kah-ree-see-mah.)*	Querida. *(Kehreedah.)*
Mon trésor. *(Mon traizawr.)*	Tesoro. *(Teh-soro.)*	Preciosa. *(Prethioh-ssa.)*
Petit bout de fesse. *(Ptee bood fess.)*	Dolcezza mia. *(Dol-cheh-tzah mee-ah.)*	Bollito de nata. *(Bohllytoh deh nátah.)*
Ma colombe. *(Mar kolombb.)*	Tortorella. *(Tor-to-reh-lah.)*	Tortolita linda. *(Tortoleetah leendah.)*
Ma poupée chérie. *(Mar poopay shairee.)*	Fatta per amare. *(Fah-tah per ah-mah-reh.)*	Chiquita querida. *(Tchickittah kehreedah.)*
Joli morceau. *(Sholee morsaw.)*	Fatalona. *(Fah-tah-lo-nah.)*	Tormento mío. *(Torméntoh meeyoh.)*

RASH STATEMENTS

I long for you.

Ich sehne mich nach Dir.

(Ish zehne mish naach dir.)

I dream of your kisses.

Ich träume von Deinen Küssen.

(Ish troyme von dynen kussen.)

I'm crazy about you.

Ich bin ganz verrückt nach Dir.

(Ish bin gaans ferrueckt naach dir.)

Come into my arms.

Komm' in meine Arme.

(Komm in myne arme.)

I'm desperate when you're away.

Ich bin verzweifelt, wenn Du nicht bei mir bist.

(Ish bin fer-tsvyfelt, ven doo nisht by mir bist.)

You are the most beautiful girl in the world.

Du bist die schönste Frau der Welt.

(Doo bist di shoenste frao der velt.)

You aren't like other women.

Du bist so ganz anders als die Anderen.

(Doo bis gans aanders aals di aanderen.)

FRENCH	ITALIAN	SPANISH
Je me consume pour vous.	Io ti bramo	Suspiro por tí.
(Sher mer consim poor voo.)	*(Ee-oh tee brah-moh.)*	*(Soospeeroh pór tee.)*
Je rêve de vos (tes) baisers.	Mi sogno i tuoi baci.	Sueño con tus besos.
(Sher raiv der vo (tay) baizay.)	*(Mee soh-nee-oh ee too-oh-ee bah-chee.)*	*(Swényoh kón toos bésoss.)*
Je suis fou de vous. (Vous me rendez fou.)	Sono pazzo per te.	Estoy loco por tí.
(Sher swee foo der voo. (Voom randay foo.))	*(Soh-noh pah-tzoh per teh.)*	*(Stóy lókoh pór tee.)*
Viens dans mes bras!	Vieni nelle mie braccia.	Ven a mis brazos.
(Vyan dan may brah!)	*(Vee-eh-nee nehl-leh mee-eh brah-cha.)*	*(Bén ah mees bráthoss.)*
Je languis loin de vous. (Je me sens perdu chaque fois que vous partez.)	Quando non ci sei, sono disperato.	Me desespero cuando estás lejos.
(Sher languee lwan der voo. (Sherm san perdi shack fwar ker voo partay.))	*(Kwandoh non chee seh-ee, soh-noh dee-speh-rah-toh.)*	*(Meh desespéroh kwándoh stás léhhos.)*
Vous êtes (tu es) la plus belle fille du monde!	Sei la piú bella ragazza del mondo.	Eres la chica más guapa del mundo.
(Voo zait (ti ay) la pli bell feey di mond!)	*(Seh-ee lah pew bellah rah-gah-tzah dehl mon-doh.)*	*(Éres lah cheekah máss gwáppah dél moondoh.)*
Vous n'êtes (tu n'es) pas comme les autres femmes.	Tu sei diversa dalle altre donne.	No eres como las demás mujeres.
(Voo nait (ti nay) par com lay zotr famm.)	*(Too seh-ee dee-ver-sah dahl-leh altreh don-neh.)*	*(Noh éres kómoh lass dehmáss moohhéress.)*

BREAKING UP

I'll write soon.

Ich schreibe bald.

(Ish shrybe baald.)

It's not going to work out, is it?

Es wird wohl doch nichts mit uns, wie?

(Es vird vohl doch nishts mit oons, vi?)

We both realize it can't last.

Es ist nicht von Dauer, das sehen wir.

(Es ist nisht fon daoer, daas zehen vir.)

I think you have someone else.

Ich glaube, Du hast jemand anderen.

(Ish glaobe, doo haast yemaand aandern.)

You don't like me anymore, do you?

Du hast mich nicht mehr gern, nicht wahr?

(Doo haast mish nisht mayr gairn, nisht vaar?)

So long; you bore me.

Zieh' Leine. Du langweilst mich.

(Tsi' lyne, doo laangvylst mish.)

FRENCH	ITALIAN	SPANISH
Je t'écrirai très prochainement. *(Sher teckreeray tray proshaïmman.)*	Scriverò presto. *(Scree-veh-ròh presto.)*	Te escribiré pronto. *(Teh screebeeréh próntoh.)*
J'ai bien peur que ça ne va pas marcher entre nous, tu crois pas? *(Shay byan pehr ker sahn va par marshay antre noo, ti crwar par?)*	Evidentemente non siamo fatti l'uno per l'altro. *(Evidenteh-mehnteh non see-amoh fah-tee l'oonoh per l'ahl-troh.)*	Esto no va a dar buen resultado, ¿verdad? *(Estoh noh báh ah dárr bwén resooltádoh, behrdád?)*
Tout comme moi, tu te rends bien compte que ça ne peut pas durer. *(Too comm mwar, tit ran byan kont ker sahn per par diray.)*	Lo sappiamo che non può durare. *(Loh sah-pee-ah-mo keh non pwo doo-rah-reh.)*	Los dos sabemos que no puede seguir. *(Lóss dóss sahbémoss ké noh pwéddeh sehgeerr.)*
Je suis persuadé que tu as quelqu'un d'autre. *(Sher swee pairsiahday ker ti ar kelkan dawtr.)*	Sento che c'è qualcun altro. *(Sent-o keh chay kwal-koon ahl-troh.)*	Creo que tienes a otro. *(Kréoh ké teeyénness ah ótroh.)*
D'ailleurs, tu ne m'aimes plus, dis-le. *(Dahyer, ti ner maim par, dee-ler.)*	Non ti piaccio piú, nevvero? *(Non tee pee-ah-cho pew, neh-vehro?)*	Ya no te gusto ¿verdad? *(Yáh noh teh goostoh, Berdath?)*
Tire-toi, tu m'embêtes! *(Teer-twar, ti mambait!)*	Vattene, mi hai stufato. *(Vah-teh-neh, me ah-y stoofah-to.)*	¡Lárgate! Estoy harto de ti. *(Lárgah-teh! Stóy árrtoh dé tee.)*

PROPOSING

Darling, will you marry me?

Liebling, willst Du mich heiraten?

(Libling, villst doo mish hyraaten?)

Will you come away with me?

Willst Du mit mir kommen?

(Villst doo mit mir kommen?)

Would you like to see my tattoos?

Komm' mit, ich zeige Dir meine Tätowierung.

(Komm mit, ish tsyge dir myne taytoviroong.)

How about it?

Wie wär's?

(Vi vair's?)

How long have I hungered for you; may I bite you?

Ich habe so nach Dir gehungert; ich muss Dich beissen.

(Ish haabe zo naach dir gehoongert; ish mooss dish byssen.)

Let's make it legal.

Aber legal.

(Aaber legaal.)

FRENCH	ITALIAN	SPANISH
Chérie, veux-tu m'épouser?	Tesoro, mi vuoi sposare?	¿Quieres casarte conmigo, querida?
(Shairee, ver-ti mai-poozay?)	(Teh-soh-roh, mee voo-oh-ee spoh-sah-reh?)	(Keeyéress kahsárr-teh kón-meegoh, kehreedah?)
Partirez-vous avec moi?	Vuoi venire via con me?	¿Quieres marcharte conmigo?
(Parteeray-voo aveck mwar?)	(Voo-oh-ee veh-nee-reh vee-ah con meh?)	(Keeyéress marchárteh kón-meegoh?)
Vous venez voir mes tatouages?	Vuoi venire a vedere i miei tatuaggi?	¿Quieres venir, y verás mis tatuajes?
(Voo vnay vwahr may tartooahsh?)	(Voo-oh-ee veh-nee-reh ah veh-deh-reh ee mee-eh-ee tah-too-ah-jee?)	(Keeyéress behneer ee behráss miss tattooáhhess?)
Alors?	Che ne diresti?	¿Qué te parece?
(Alohr?)	(Keh neh dee-reh-stee?)	(Ké teh parétheh?)
J'ai faim de toi—je peux te mordre?	Ti potrei mangiare—lascia che ti dia un morsetto.	Tengo hambre de ti, ¿puedo morderte?
(Shay fam der twar—sher per ter mordr?)	(Tee poh-treh-ee man-ja-reh—lah-shee-ah keh tee dee-ah oon mor-set-toh.)	(Téngoh ámbreh dé tee, pwéddoh mohrdérr-teh?)
On va régulariser la chose, veux-tu?	Rendiamo la cosa legale.	Hagámoslo legal.
(On va raiggilareezay la shawz, ver-ti?)	(Rehn-dee-ah-moh lah koh-zah leh-gah-leh.)	(Aghámoss-loh legál.)

PROPOSING

Marriage is so old-fashioned, but do you want to give it a try?

Heiraten ist altmodisch, aber willst Du es nicht einmal probieren?

(Hyraaten ist altmodish, aaber villst doo es nisht ynmaal probiren?)

Intelligent people like us don't need ceremonies.

Eine Feier brauchen wir nicht, dazu sind wir zu vernünftig.

(Yne fyer braochen vir nisht, datsoo zind vir tsoo fernuenftig.)

When?

Wann?

(Vaann?)

IF SHE SAYS NO

Why not?

Warum nicht?

(Varoom nisht?)

Don't be old-fashioned.

Sei doch nicht so altmodisch.

(Zy doch nisht zo altmodish.)

FRENCH	ITALIAN	SPANISH

Le mariage est une institution démodée, je sais bien, mais si on essayait un peu?

(Ler mareeahs aitin ansteetisyon daimoday, sher say byan, may see on essaiyay an per?)

Il matrimonio è un'istituzione antiquata, ma vuoi fare una prova?

(Eel mah-tree-moh-nee-oh eh oon ee-stee-too-tzee-ohnéh antee-kwah-tah, mah voo-oh-eee fah-reh oo-nah pro-vah?)

Casarse está pasado de moda, pero podríamos hacer un ensayo.

(Kasárr-seh stáh passádoh deh módah, péroh podreeyamoss athérr oon ensáhyoh.)

Nous sommes bien trop raisonnables pour avoir besoin d'une cérémonie, n'est-ce pas?

(Noo somm byan tro raizonabl poor avwahr berzwan din sairaimonee, naice-par?)

Ma siamo persone troppo intelligenti per avere bisogno di una cerimonia.

(Mah see-ah-moh per-sohneh trop-poh intel-lee-jehntee per ah-ver bee-zoh-neeoh dee oo-nah chairee-mohnee-ah.)

Somos demasiado sensibles para necesitar una ceremonia.

(Sómoss demmasyádoh senseeb-less párah nethessittárr oonah zerehmón-yah.)

Quand?

(Kan?)

Quando?

(Kwan-doh?)

¿Cuándo?

(Kwándoh?)

Pourquoi pas?

(Poorkwar par?)

Perchè no?

(Per-keh noh?)

¿Por qué no?

(Pór ké noh?)

Qu'est-ce que tu peux être vieux jeu!!!

(Kaisker ti per zaitr vyer sher!!!)

Non essere cosí all'antica.

(Non ehs-seh-reh koh-zée ahl-lan-tee-kah.)

¡No seas anticuada!

(Noh sé-ass antikwádda!)

IF SHE SAYS NO

Everybody else does.

Jeder macht es doch so.
(Yeder maacht es doch zo.)

Nobody will know.

Braucht doch niemand zu wissen.
(Braocht doch nimaant tsoo vissen.)

The place is empty.

Est ist kein Mensch hier.
(Es ist kyn mensh hir.)

Don't torment me.

Quäle mich nicht.
(Quayle mish nisht.)

But I *do* love you.

Aber ich liebe Dich doch.
(Aaber ish lihbe dish doch.)

REASONS

I can't marry you; my wife would object.

Ich kann Dich nicht heiraten, meine Frau würde es nicht erlauben.

(Ish kann dish nisht hyraaten, myne frao vuerde es nisht erlaoben.)

FRENCH	ITALIAN	SPANISH

Tout le monde le fait.
(Tool mond ler fay.)

Lo fanno tutti.
(Loh fahn-noh toot-tee.)

Todo el mundo lo hace.
(Tóddoh él moondoh loh átheh.)

Personne n'en saura rien.
(Pairsonn nan sawrah ryan.)

Non lo saprà nessuno.
(Non loh sah-práh nehs-soo-noh.)

Nadie lo sabrá.
(Náddye loh sahbráh.)

Il n'y a personne ici.
(Eel nyar pairsonn eecee.)

Non c'è nessuno.
(Non-chèh nes-soo-noh.)

Este lugar está desierto.
(Ésteh loogárr stáh dess-yértoh.)

Ne me tourmente pas.
(Ner mer toormant par.)

Non tormentarmi.
(Non tor-mentar-mee.)

No me atormentes más.
(Noh mé attorméntess máss.)

Mais *bien sûr* que je t'aime!
(May byan sir kersh taim!)

Ma sí che ti amo.
(Mah seè keh tee ah-moh.)

Pero es que te amo.
(Péroh ess ké teh ámoh.)

Je ne peux pas t'épouser, ma femme n'aimerait pas du tout ça!

(Shern per par taipoozay, ma famm naimray par di too sah!)

Non posso sposarti, mia moglie sarebbe contraria.

(Non po-soh spo-sahr-tee, mee-ah mo-lee-eh sah-reh-bbeh con-trah-ree-ah.)

No puedo casarme contigo, porque mi esposa se opondría.

(Nó pwéddoh kassárr-meh kón-teegoh, pór-ké mee spóssah sé ohpóndreeyah.)

REASONS

I can't marry you because I'm too young.

Ich kann Dich nicht heiraten, weil ich zu jung bin.

(Ish kann dish nisht hyraaten, vyl ish tsoo yoong bin.)

I can't marry you because I'm a fugitive.

Ich kann Dich nicht heiraten, ich bin flüchtig.

(Ish kann dish nisht hyraaten, ish bin flueshtig.)

I can't marry you because I'm underage.

Ich kann Dich nicht heiraten, weil ich noch unmündig bin.

(Ish kann dish nisht hyraaten, vyl ish noch oonmuendig bin.)

I can't marry you because of my war wound.

Ich kann Dich nicht heiraten wegen meiner Kriegsverletzung.

(Ish kann dish nisht hyraaten vegen myner kriegsferletsung.)

I can't marry you because I'm too poor.

Ich kann Dich nicht heiraten, weil ich zu arm bin.

(Ish kann dish nisht hyraaten, vyl ish tsoo arm bin.)

FRENCH	ITALIAN	SPANISH
Je ne peux pas t'épouser, je suis trop jeune. *(Shern per par taipoozay, sher swee tro shern.)*	Non posso sposarti, sono troppo giovane. *(Non po-soh spo-sahr-tee, sono tro-poh joh-vah-neh.)*	No puedo casarme contigo porque soy demasiado joven. *(Nó pwéddoh kassárr-meh kón-teegoh, pór-ké sóy dehmassyadoh hóbben.)*
Je ne peux pas t'épouser, je suis en fuite pour l'instant. *(Shern per par taipoozay, sher sweezan fweet poor lanstan.)*	Non posso sposarti, sono un evaso. *(Non po-soh spo-sahr-tee, sono oon eh-vah-so.)*	No puedo casarme contigo porque soy un fugitivo. *(Nó pwéddoh kassárr-meh kón-teegoh, pór-ké sóy oon foohheetíboh.)*
Tu ne peux pas épouser un mineur que je sache! *(Tin per par zaipoozay an meenehr ker sher sash!)*	Non posso sposarti, sono minorenne. *(Non po-soh spo-sahr-tee, sono mee-noh-reh-neh.)*	No puedo casarme contigo porque soy menor de edad. *(Nó pwéddoh kassárr-meh kón-teegoh, pór-ké sóy mehnórr deh eddád.)*
Il m'est impossible de t'épouser à cause de mes blessures de guerre. *(Eel may tamposeebl der taipoozay ar cawz der may blessir der gair.)*	Non posso sposarti a causa della mia ferita di guerra. *(Non po-soh spo-sahr-tee, ah cah-oo-sah-deh-lah mee-a feh-ree-tah dee gweh-rah.)*	No puedo casarme contigo por mi herida de guerra. *(Nó pwéddoh kassárr-meh kón-teegoh, pór mee ehreedah deh ghérrah.)*
Je ne peux pas t'épouser, je suis trop pauvre. *(Shern per par taipoozay, sher swee tro pawvr.)*	Non posso sposarti, sono troppo povero. *(Non po-soh spo-sahr-tee, sono tro-poh poh-veh-ro.)*	No puedo casarme contigo porque soy demasiado pobre. *(Nó pwéddoh kassárr-meh kón-teegoh, pór-ké sóy dehmassyádoh póbbreh.)*

MORE USEFUL WORDS

Ravishing.	Hinreissend.
	(Hinryssend.)
Beautiful.	Schön.
	(Shoen.)
Bed.	Bett.
	(Bett.)
Lovely.	Reizend.
	(Rytsend.)
Exquisite.	Grosse Klasse.
	(Grosse klasse.)
Couch.	Sofa.
	(Zofa.)
Superb.	Hervorragend.
	(Herfor-raagend.)
Dazzling.	Verwirrend.
	(Fervirrend.)
Chaise Longue.	Chaise-longue.
	(Chaise-longue.)

FRENCH	ITALIAN	SPANISH
Ravissant. *(Raveesant.)*	Affascinante. *(Ah-fah-shee-nahn-teh.)*	Arrebatadora. *(Ahrrehbahtahdórah.)*
Beau (Belle) *(Bo (Bell).)*	Bella. *(Beh-llah.)*	Hermosa. *(Ehrmóssah.)*
Un lit. *(An lee.)*	Letto. *(Leh-to.)*	Cama. *(Kámah.)*
Mignon (Mignonne). *(Meenyonn.)*	Incantevole. *(In-cahn-teh-voleh.)*	Cariñosa. *(Karynyóssa.)*
Exquis (Exquise). *(Exkee (Exkeez).)*	Deliziosa. *(Deh-lee-tzeeo-sah.)*	Exquisita. *(Exkeeseetah.)*
Un divan. *(An deevan.)*	**Sofá.** *(Sofah.)*	Sofá. *(Sofah.)*
Superbe. *(Sipairb.)*	Meravigliosa. *(Meh-rah-vee-lee-o-sah.)*	Soberbia. *(Sobérbeeyah.)*
Eblouissant (Eblouissante). *(Ebblweesan (Ebblweesant).)*	Splendente. *(Splehn-dehnteh.)*	Deslumbrante. *(Dessloombránteh.)*
Un récamier. *(An recahmyay.)*	Sedia a sdraio. *(Seh-deeah ah sdrah-yo.)*	Tumbona. *(Toombónah.)*